THE LIVING STARS

DR ERIC MORSE

AMETHYST BOOKS
NEW YORK LONDON

Published in the United States by
Amethyst Books, P.O. Box 895,
Woodstock N.Y.12498
and in the United Kingdom by
Amethyst Books, 44 Gledstanes Road,
London W14

Designed by Paperweight.

Library of Congress Catalog Card Number:
87–072725

ISBN 0–944256–02–3

Amethyst Books are distributed in the United States by Publishers Group West, 4065 Hollis, Emeryville CA 94608 and in the United Kingdom by Ashgrove Distribution, 4 Brassmill Centre, Brassmill Lane, Bath BA1 3JN.

To Kim and Poppy

May God, All Gracious, All Merciful
Bless them Eternally for coming into
My Life and bringing Me closer to Him

Grateful Acknowledgements

No author of a work like this one can ever be sure that he has said adequate thanks to all who have helped him in his labours. This is especially so when he has been so long aware of worlds of living souls beyond that event we call death, so many of whom give of their love and inspiration modestly with no attempt to make known their former mortal identities, whether famous or obscure. For all of them I thank All Gracious God that they are Blessed by His Great Mercy to have been able and willing to inspire me. To my recently passed wife Kim and her sweet friend in mortal life and beyond it I have dedicated this inadequate tribute to their memory, and I know they have not asked even that small recognition of their comfort and loving support.

Of friends here in mortal life with me I should like to mention my co-author of *The Dark Stars*, Bernard Fitzwalter, without whose encouragement to join him in that work I should probably never have carried out my long-held intent of writing this one. Also Dr Boris Kamenko, my astronomer friend for his tireless work on Phaeton. I thank also my publisher and friend Nicholas Bamforth for asking me to do this, and for his sympathy and patience after the passing of Kim and my delay in completing this work. I cannot miss thanking also our friend Debbie Kopelmann who brought us together. And thank, I must, another in the immortal worlds, her son Danny, but for whom she and I would not have met. Then let me thank Caroll for her long urging to me to get on with this book, as also did many in the Astrological Lodge of London, and finally a host of fellow students who made me see how much a work of this kind has been needed.

ERIC MORSE

Contents

Introduction

'This really is a discovery of the greatest importance: We now know why it is that only some stars shine with constant brightness while others vary . . . . . .'

How many millions of people have heard a popular figure in astronomy say something like that on T.V., and how many thousands of them have said: 'What, pray, is *important* about the behaviour of a *star* billions of miles away in space?'

A lively debate then ensues among those interested – usually most of those present – as to whether the matter really *is* important, or just interesting for those who like that kind of thing. Even the few who protest they have 'something better to think about' can rarely tear themselves away from the company but feel they must remain to say things like 'God put us on this *Earth*, not on *Polaris* or *Aldebaran*', or 'If God kept His explosions out there among the stars instead of letting wars and earthquakes happen here, perhaps I could believe in Him'. Somehow, God always gets drawn in to such a debate, in the role of the defendant, with this strictly Earthbound humanitarian to prosecute Him and opening the case by asserting that He doesn't exist anyway! While the astronomer may possibly become so absorbed in the chemistry and physics of the stars that he puts philosophy aside –

and in fact few can do so for very long – the layman asks much more readily: 'How do the stars and the Universe relate to *me*? Where am I in all that?' The less of an astrologer or theologian our humanitarian is, the more vehemently does he or she demand answer to these astrological and theological questions!

So, in some strange way, the stars really wield an influence upon us. That is not to say that they have some instrumentally measurable effect by reason of their colours, brilliance, chemistry, distances or apparent locations in our night sky; all of that is a matter for other considerations then we are talking of just now. Our simple case for the moment is to say that the stars influence us because they are there, and will not go away. There they are, superior to any wish we might have in the matter, a sight of beauty to many, to others a reassuring sign that there is a 'Power' greater than Man, and One which has its own evident concept of order and stability; to yet others this very suggestion of a greater Presence is something disconcerting in so many ways. It may remind them that other men are spending fortunes on 'space' while people are poor on Earth, that a star lives immensely longer than a human, whose existence may not be so important as we have esteemed it after all, and that there doesn't seem to be anyone reliable that we can ask about this awesome thought. And then again; if there is such an authority, who can answer, what are we to make of that? Worse still, what does it make of us? The old notions, mostly fears, of some Supreme Being with an eye cocked critically in our direction, come flooding back to us from a past we thought we had left comfortably behind in our modern age of Man as the sole ruler over his own fate.

And if that fate should then include some reckoning in a 'hereafter', a notion which some find comforting to believe in, should they really be so happy about that? The atheist may actually feel happier in his conviction that there is NO hereafter, at least while he is young and not facing the question as an imminent one, except that the splendid display of the stars hints to him that he could be very, very wrong!

So the stars are as living to him as to the truest of the Faithful, to whom they are like friendly companions who accompany one on the long walk home down the dark lane. To our atheist they are more like that man whom we are sure is following us with sinister intent, but who is quite innocently taking the same path to his own home farther on.

Tody we are not the primitive, cave-dwelling man we hear of so much, fearful of all the forces of Nature, gazing abjectly upwards to the bright 'holes in the heavens', through which he hopes the gods are looking favourably down upon him, not understanding that the 'holes' are in reality other stars like our nearby Sun. Yet still do we fear Nature in its violent moments and still do we maintain large bodies of exalted persons at the heads of our 'religions', whose job it is to help us relate to gods or to the ONE GOD whom many people still feel instinctively to be somewhere up there beyond those stars.

In the West, especially, we suffer much conflict about this: Show too much belief in this Deity and one may actually be thought to be in need of 'care', too little and one may be suspected of revolutionary politics; show any respect for the ancient doctrine that the planets and stars are any kind of 'Sign' from that Deity, and astronomer and church minister alike may well descend in wrath or contempt upon the errant astrologer. All three may find themselves standing together next Sunday to sing:

> Praise the Lord; ye Heavens adore Him;
> Praise Him Angels in the Height;
> Sun and Moon bow down before Him;
> Praise Him all ye Stars and Light.

It goes without saying, of course, that the same minister of church will in due season deliver lectures to the very young, of how three astrologers (wise men, kings) followed a guiding star to the stable where the founder figure of his religion was born; and monarch, prime minister, president and most other 'top people' will also celebrate this event with its very astrological component. The stars are such a living force in us in other ways too that we use the word 'star' for anyone who attains fame among us in sport and entertainment.

So we conclude this introduction and now look at the strange story of how Man first came to his extraordinary sense of relationship with the stars. It is very different to the commonly taught notion of that primitive savage with the vocabulary of one word 'Ugh'. And then in the chapters that follow we shall see what kinds of relationship he has built with the Living Stars.

CHAPTER 1

Disaster – The Great Catastrophe

The two titles of this chapter are both commonly used words in our modern language but few who use them stop to notice that both are of an astronomical connonation; still fewer appreciate that both point back in time to the dramatic event which was the origin of all Man's sense of personal relationship with the stars.

The word 'Disaster' means 'no star' or 'loss of star' just as, for example, 'disunity' means 'no unity' or 'loss of unity'. Our other word, 'Catastrophe', means 'Fall of a star'.

And both words have their origin, not in observations of supernovae or similar cosmic explosions far out in space, but in one particular such event very close indeed to planet Earth. And this did not happen millions of years ago, as all the great events that formed our planet of today are generally said to have occured, but as recently as about 8,500 B.C. In his remarkable book, 'The End of Atlantis', Dr. Otto Muck gives the precise date as June 5th, 8498 B.C., at 8 p.m.! We may well raise a suspicious eyebrow at such precision (Was it by Julian or Gregorian calendar, G.M.T. or some other timing?) but we cannot dismiss the late Dr. Muck as some kind of freak. A celebrated physicist and engineer of the 1940s, he was quite sane enough to be the inventor of the 'schnorkel' by which means submarines could draw air from the surface while travelling underwater, and he was also a prominent member of Germany's rocket research centre at Peenemunde, to which so much of our current space technology, in all countries, owes a considerable debt. (And note also that 'considerable' is yet another word of astronomical origins: *Lit* 'With the stars'.)

The same story of a stellar explosion very close to Earth and its neighbouring planets is also told in works of much earlier writers: the Romans Ovid and Manilius, the Greeks Plato and Nonnos, the Hindu Vedas, and even earlier well-preserved accounts from cultures in south-west Africa and Polynesia. By the Romans and Greeks the ill-fated star was called Phaethon, or Phaeton, the name revived for it in the 1950s-60s by Soviet researchers tracing its after-effects on Earth, and, in 'Hamlet's Mill' by Santillana & von Dechend, there is an excellent chapter on all the ancient versions of the story. Most recently, Bernard Fitzwalter and Raymond Henry have treated it especially for present-day astrologers in 'The Dark Stars'.

Extracting the main features from the varied poetry and mythology, we find that, until about 8500 B.C., there were two suns in our local sky, of which only one now remains and is appropriately named Solus or Sol – 'alone' in the 'Solar' system.

Such a pair of stars close together is called a Binary Pair, not to be confused with a 'Double' when two stars far apart simply look to be close as seen from Earth. True binaries are not uncommon in space and are well-known as sources of Nova explosions. What happens then is that one of the pair, usually the smaller, has sucked material from the partner until the gravitational field of the latter can no longer contain the internal pressures of its nuclear furnace. The result is a gigantic atomic explosion destroying the star partially or totally. All that we see from Earth, even with big telescopes, is a very bright light for a few weeks or months, as though a star has just been created – hence the name Nova (New) given to it. But, on a planet near to the striken star, the destruction is horrific.

Conservative estimates at our distance in time from the event suggest that Phaeton exploded with such force that practically nothing was left of it; some commentators think the asteriod Ceres, notably dense and nearly a perfect sphere, may be the core remnant of the star, and this seems the more likely since the present author and a colleague calculated independently positions for the 'ghost' of Phaeton today which are close both to each other and to that of Ceres, even though neither of us had used the asteriod in our reckoning. Of the thousands of other rocks in the Asteriod Belt, we consider these to be remnants both of Phaeton and of probable planets totally destroyed by it. The strange presence of a seemingly 'inner' type planet, Pluto, at a mean distance from the Sun greater than that of Neptune, but in a very mis-shapen and over-tilted orbit, suggests that it may have been flung out there by the star's explosion.

The craters which cover Mercury and Luna, our present moon, and the desolation on Mars, which people over centuries have insisted either is or should be inhabited, along with the evidence of vast craters here on Earth, which are mainly hidden by our oceans – all reveal just the kind of damage we should expect from a Nova less than twice as far from us as is the Sun.

The legendary stories of the loss of the continent of Atlantis, and of Lemuria too, are all part of the same event, better examined by von Muck than we have space for here, while some quite sound commentators have included the vanished Lilith, the smaller moon which Earth had before Luna, as about the right size of missile to have sunk two continents and changed Earth's rotational axis so much that regions once tropical are now found buried under temperate and even icy polar regions of the planet. In his book 'Le Paradis perdu de Mu' (The lost Paradise of Mu (=Lemuria), the distinguished French academician Louis-Claude Vincent finds that our equator once ran roughly along the present north-south meridians of Stockholm and Capetown. Hindu vedic accounts in the Mahabharata, supported by Tibetan records and even by some hints in the Judaeo-Christian Old Testament, tell how once we had one moon, then two, then only one again – the new one – and how the Sun stood still, then went the other way. All these are all such probable phenomena during such a catastrophe that there is no reason not to believe them when so much else supports the basic event.

For the rest of the story, von Muck and others contend that Earth was showered with radioactive debris that destroyed most of animal life almost overnight, accounting for herds of mammoths dying just where they stood, to be iced in for centuries as Earth's axis tilted, while a huge pall of black cloud blotted out light from all but a narrow band near our present equator for some fifteen hundred years. Our very common fear of darkness is not easy to explain unless it is something not natural to us, yet all our great religions speak of it as of an evil from which we must be saved: 'Seek ye the Light'; 'I am the Light of the World'; 'The People that walked in Darkness have seen a Great Light' - The quotations are endless in all creeds.

But it is explicable if we once lived on a planet where night was not known, as on a planet suspended between two suns, so that it never knew anything dimmer than a brief twilight between their risings and settings in turn.

What would life have been like on Earth in that situation, which we still speak of as the Golden Age? We can say little of it for sure, but we can safely say that those ancestors of ours were not at all primitive or living in caves. Old legends tell of wonderful palaces and other great edifices of engineering, legends told among peoples whose kings, even, lived in comparative hovels. So whence came such tales if not from long handed-down accounts or else from underlying memories in the tribal or wider human psyche? The high culture of the Golden Age and the Atlantean civilisation must have existed, and it must have been much superior in quality to the Minoan society of around 1750 B.C., whose own demise by the volanic explosion of the island of Thera has caused some scholars to confuse it with Atlantis.

One thing our Atlantean ancestors would have lacked, however, unless some few of them really did have means of space travel, would have been our awareness of the millions of stars beyond our little patch of the Universe. We do not see stars in daylight; neither did they. But they did not see them by night either, for they had no night. A few legends tell that they knew of just one or two bright stars, Sirius and Vega being possible cases, which showed up in their twilight hour just as a careful observer may see them in fading daylight today, as we may sometimes also see Venus, Mercury and Jupiter by twilight. But one or two briefly seen stars give no idea of the vast Universe that we know of.

Then came the great catastrophe. One of their two suns, diminishing in size, began to emit a long snake of flame towards the other, and that fiery snake or dragon, common to so many ancient myths, worked its way slowly but inexorably nearer to Earth. It may well have scorched the life off other planets first, for there is no reason to assert that Earth was the only bearer of intelligent life in the binary system of that era, and it must be counted possible that some inhabitants had developed limited space travel at least, and would effect a timely escape. Again we have too many legends of strangers descending from the skies to dismiss them all.

Here on Earth there was probably no escape, even if some few did have means of space travel. Where would they go when refugees from elsewhere were already arriving here? The 'Mahabharata' tells of a terrible war here at the same time, fought with very high technology and with terrible destruction. We are left uncertain as to whether it was between us and the arrivals from other planet(s) or among ourselves for the safest refuges available, or thought to be safe. At all events, when Phaeton reached the zodiacal degree later said to be nineteen of Scorpio by Roman and Greek retelling from earlier records, the impoverished star exploded. Or, as the later legends put it, Jupiter (Zeus) hit it with a thunderbolt to save the Earth. The degree is still called 'Serpentis', 'of the snake', by astrologers and counted about the most malefic point in the zodiac. Strangely, the star *north scale* of Libra, alias *north claw* of Scorpio, on this same degree of 'Serpentis' is associated with high intelligence in us, and we shall have an idea why very shortly. The degree given, by the way, is in astrology's traditional 'tropical' zodiac; the 'true' position by sidereal reckoning at the present time is twenty-four of Libra.

CHAPTER 2

After the Show

At three degrees of the Scorpion, the fiery serpent streaked forth and Phaeton began his headlong fall towards Earth; so goes the tale as told by the poets. It was not in fact Earth but Sun that Phaeton was really heading for: Earth just happened to be in the way of the falling star, which disintegrated sixteen days later – just in time to avert total destruction of the planet. By some other accounts, the explosion occurred at three Scorpio; the first debris hit Earth at nineteen, sinking Atlantis. It is not very important which is the more accurate.

Nor need we ponder long as to what is meant by Jupiter's bolt that saved our planet. It may have been another planet in the path; it may actually have been a dislodged moon of the planet Jupiter; it could have been our moon Lilith, which later retellings have included in the story in the most confusing manner. The qabalistic work 'Sepher Yezirah', for example, of about 1300 A.D., tells the mythical story of the jealousy between the two stars, in which Sun says to the ill-fated rival: 'Go and diminish thyself!', but saying it to Lilith, not to Phaeton. Apart from the nonsense of two celestial bodies in dispute like emotional humans, we cannot miss the absurdity of a tiny satellite like Lilith, no brighter than Venus at best, being classed as one of 'Two Great Lights' in this qabalist's account. Clearly, he has let his intuition become confused between two participants in the disaster, but that does imply that Lilith indeed had a major role in it – more than just being lost to us or destroyed in space.

So, by that reckoning, it could well have been collision with Lilith that brought final destruction to Phaeton, and herself, or she may have been the missile that plunged to Earth and sank Atlantis. For the one reason or the other, Lilith has had a bad name ever since as the fiend of the night, destroyer of children, and other evils too numerous to mention here. Barbara Black Koltuv's little 'Book of Lilith' is excellent on the folklore of the 'demonic lady' side of Lilith, including the Sepher Yezirah material; a worthwhile work on the astronomy or astrology of our former moon has yet to appear.

But, in this chapter, we must be mostly concerned with the aftermath of the disaster for life on Earth, human life especially. How did we survive at all, in what state and with what long-term results? The short answers to the triple question are: 'Only just'; 'Awful'; 'Astounding'.

Even if Phaeton was at its nominal distance – twice that of the Sun – from Earth when it exploded, the radiation flash fifteen minutes later would have been nearly instant death to anyone exposed to it. If it had already come as close to Earth as Lilith, 600,000 miles (960,000 km), then Earth itself must have been tossed like a cork in the ocean.

The mystery of sudden death overtaking mammoths and dinosaurs just where they stood, herded to drink or graze, is a mystery no longer. The 'Mahabharata' tells of elephants charging for the rivers, their skins ablaze; others, mercifully, died quicker than that, but the dinosaur herds' remains in river valleys tell the same tragic tale.

In such a holocaust, smaller creatures must have been incinerated and left no traces for us to dig up except in isolated sheltered places, and these must have included mankind. This is the reason that it is not much believed that men ever met dinosaurs, even though some of our oldest heraldic art and many findings of cave drawings and paintings clearly imply that we did know such creatures. Modern archeologists are also baffled that they find remains of a flat-skulled humanoid creature which seems altogether too primitive to have produced arts such as some of those paintings truly are, while they have found almost none that they feel were capable of a civilised way of life. So, they portray these 'men' as hairy neo-apes in our museums, and still they look for a 'missing link' between these and apes as we know them today.

They are seeking what never existed, looking for proof of evolution by a pattern which never happened, and letting their precious method of 'carbon dating' mislead them utterly about the historical period of the remains they find. Their calculations of radioactive decay do not take account of the massive irradiation of the planet by Phaeton nor of the upheavals then (not X million years earlier) in Earth's surface structure down to very great depths, when 'the Fountains of the Great Deep were all broken up' (Genesis VII, 11).

So let us set the record a little nearer to the probable truth; we do not promise better than that. Those flat-skulled humanoids were not club-wielding savages in animal skins, at least not before Phaeton exploded. They lacked our cortical brain structure, yes, but that did not deny them the intelligence needed for a high civilisation.

Old stories, from the Bible and like sources, tell of Man 'walking and talking with God', and some also tell of Man being able to talk with the birds and animals too. These stories should not be taken to be just poetic allegory, as it has become the custom to 'interpret' them over the past three centuries; religions today have grown weak and confused, precisely because their ministers no longer believe their own literature to be literal, the ministers being themselves products of the agnostic society to which they still try to preach their faith.

Those old stories may be much more literally true than we commonly believe, however, when the biological condition of Man before the Great Disaster is recognised. His nervous system and intelligence then had its centre in the Cerebellum, the highly efficient brain at the base of our skull whose functions we little understand today. There is no doubt, however, that apart from managing much of our seemingly automatic body workings, it also manages our psychic functioning – not just the remarkable E.S.P. which some people manifest, but also that state we all find ourselves in at times when we just seem to *know* what to do, or how it is going to be, without having calculated it or been taught it through the cerebral cortex.

Ante-Diluvian mankind, in common with other creatures, had only the cerebellum as the summit of the nervous system, and shared a common psychic awareness with all other animal life around him. To have told him this would have been neaningless to him, for he knew of no other state in which one could be. He would not have thought about God as Something or Someone with whom he should seek contact; not having evolved a separated cortex, he knew nothing of 'sin' – that state of lonely separation from the Source of Life which only evolved as the inevitable concomitant of the cortex, itself a mutation brought about by the explosion of Phaeton and the damage done on Earth.

But, the event having happened, Man was in 'treble trouble'. First the sheer terror of it, then the fifteen hundred years of sickness during which life-span shortened, from the 'nine hundred years' of Methuselah to the 'three score and ten' of the cast-out Adam – cast-out meaning precisely that he had evolved that separated cortical consciousness. And thirdly, as at last the sky came clear again, the discovery that the world was a very different place to the stories handed down to him over the past fifty or more generations. For the Universe was not a bright sky with two suns lighting it and warming the Earth evenly, but a sky with only one Sun which lit the sky for only part of the day, sometimes for long periods and with almost too much heat, at other times for only short periods so that life almost perished from the coldness.

And, when the Sun was not on view, there was this other great light, Luna, a cold light which was soon found to have curious effects upon the brain, the emotions and the sexual functioning of the body, not by any means unreservedly welcome.

And when Luna was in the sky alone (its name, like Sol for the Sun, means 'alone') as a second god or goddess who contested with the daytime one for rule over Earth and thus inspired humans to poly-theistic beliefs, there were also, far, far beyond it, thousands of other tiny lights – more gods perhaps, or else tiny holes in the dark fabric which now separated Heaven from Earth. And, through those holes, the gods kept watch on the world they had once created but no longer seemed pleased with, or perhaps it was Supreme God Himself who dwelt beyond that dark curtain, for some of the points of light were observed to move about if watched over several days, weeks and months, going back and forth, meeting each other now and then, and evidently doing something about things on Earth; for various events happened here when those 'wanderers', or 'planets', got together or separated again. They must be lesser gods and it was soon seen, by what happened here, that they did not all like us, or each other.

Caught up in the affairs of that fractious family, humans began to respond in a variety of ways. Some sought a communion with the warm Sun, for it obviously made one feel well and happy, and food grew when it warmed the soil. Others worshipped Luna, for it (she) helped humans to have offspring so that they might not become extinct. Yet others tried to come to terms with the whole 'pantheon' of planets, Sun and Luna included, for clearly we had to make some kind of pact or 'covenant' with them all.

And then yet other humans, clinging to the hope that those old stories of our erstwhile state of grace had truth in them after all, looked out to those distant stars and saw a sign in their very unmoving-ness that, beyond them, was a true GOD for Whom nothing had changed, with Whom humanity might still find harmony, peace and promise of unending Life. The planet-worshippers told stories of how Jupiter, the biggest and favourite among them, had placed certain great and heroic humans in the sky to live there eternally, and the various patterns of the stars showed them there: Hercules, Perseus, Andromeda, Bo-otes and many, many more.

What if the planet-worshippers had it slightly wrong, if in reality the True Divinity had placed those stars in such recognisable ways that men's minds, however mutated they had become, could see His entire Creation as a huge Living Family, Stars, Planets, Earth, Man and All Life, All that was, is and ever will be, all held eternally, in the wonder and joy of Life? Those *Living Stars* were His Sign to Man that this is so, and Man's stories about the heroes and heroines they represented to him were the products of that brain which still enjoyed, compressed and pushed down in the skull though it now was, a state of perfect at-onement with HIM and All His Creation.

HE, it was, Who made up those stories about the wonderful patterns in the night sky; we received them via that old brain that *knew* Him and did not just cogitate *about* him as this new cortical brain did. And if He said these were *Living Stars*, for men to take heart from, then *living* they were – and still are: For another feature of that cerebellum is that it does not forget or discard anything with the flow of time, as the cortex rightly discards the calculated guesses it has found to be less than the whole truth. That older brain does not Believe things, for a little or a long while: it KNOWS what it has been made to know, and for all time to come.

And now we shall see what it, our supremely conscious 'unconscious', *knows* about *The Living Stars*.

CHAPTER 3

Signs and Constellations

Many people are confused about these two terms in astrology and astronomy, so a few words now are needed to clear things up.

A *Constellation* is a group of stars which form a certain pattern as seen from Earth, and which men have been inspired to see as looking like some particular animal, or human, or implement made by men, or some geometrical configuration. Typical examples are *Aries*, the Ram, *Cepheus*, a famous King, *Sextans*, a mariner's Sextant, and *Crux Australis*, the Southern Cross.

Many of the Constellations we know today are of great antiquity; we say they are 'original constellations', and these have deep psychological and archtetypal significance for us. Different cultures, the Chinese, the Hindu, the Babylonian, the Arabic, Aztec and many more, have different names for them, different stories attached to them, and yet it is amazing how the variations seem to harmonise so much that an astrologer will read much the same significance of a star on a particular horoscope, no matter which culture he has followed and therefore which name and associated legend he has used. In some ancient cultures some of the stars in the constellations as we know them were treated as one-star constellations, or *Asterisms*, the Greater Dog Star, *Sirius*, being a famous example. We know it as the prime star of the *Dog* which hunts with *Orion*, who is both taking on *Taurus* the *Bull* and hunting *Lepus* the *Hare*, but to the Egyptians

Sirius was the god *Osiris*, whence in fact we get its name. And we shall find other examples like this.

The *Zodiac* is a selection of twelve particular constellations, all of them close to the Ecliptic, the plane of Earth's path round the Sun. Originally these were all representations of animals, including some human ones, whence comes the word Zodiac, or Zoo –diac, the animals of the day (or year). The only non-animal (or human) one is Libra, the Scales, or Balance, a late addition to the system at the behest of Julius Caesar, so it is said, when he had the calendar improved, Libra was carved out of Scorpio, and its two chief stars, North and South Scales (or Pans of the Scales), are also still known as the North and South Claws of the Scorpion.

The astrologer's *Zodiac*, in Western astrology but not in Indian, has another role apart from being a collection of constellations. It is also a system of *signs* giving specific qualities to planets in them.

These *signs* do not move with Time, as the *constellations* in fact do. Our Sun, taking us with it, moves 'retrograde' through the Constellations, at the rate of about one degree in 72 years; it takes 2160 years to pass through one Zodiacal Constellation, or 25,920 years to go through all twelve. The main school of Indian astrology reckons the '*sun sign*' to be the actual Constellation the Sun is in at any particular time, and this reckoning is called the *Sidereal Zodiac*. The Western Astrologer, in the Greek tradition, works by the *Tropical Zodiac*, an unvarying system of *signs* which, perhaps unfortunately, have the same names as twelve of the Constellations – because once in every 25,920 years the two systems coincide, as they last did in 217 A.D. At present (1987) O degrees of the *sign* Aries is at 5.5 of the preceding Constellation, Pisces, and in just less than 400 years the Vernal Equinox, as we call 0 Aries, will be late in Aquarius by *Sidereal*, Constellational reckoning; but still at 0 Aries by *Tropical* usage. Contrary to the mistaken opinion of some astronomers, the well taught astrologer does know about this. The *signs* he uses tell him things about a horoscope which do not alter with the passage of Time whereas

Constellations, albeit used more rarely in the West, register some very profound changes indeed.

In 2018 AD the star *Regulus*, 'Star of Kings', while still in the *constellation* of *Leo*, 'King of Beasts' where it has always been, will change *sign* from *Leo* into *Virgo*, and the unchanging qualities of the *Sign Virgo* will affect strongly the ways in which kings (most of whom have that star prominent in their horoscopes) will behave and execute their duties.

Their duties are going to take precedence over the conquest of wealth and power, or else they will not long stay kings (or other rulers of similar prestige). While still at 5 degrees of Leo by Constellation, Regulus reached the last degree of Leo by Sign in 1937, just as World War II was about to show up which monarchs were ready to serve and stand by their people and which were heading for early dethronement. Since then, it has been quite 'the thing' for monarchs, figureheads and the truly autocratic rulers alike to visit their subjects' homes and workplaces, to build hospitals and schools, to review laws unchanged for centuries, and to make ambassadorial journeys abroad to improve their nations' images and relationships in the world.

So much for kings: Hopefully the example of Regulus has shown how by *constellation* the star continues to indicate high office for someone but how, by change of *sign*, the conditions of holding that office must alter. The duty-orientated qualities of *Virgo* as a *sign* do not alter but the royal attributes of the *constellation Leo* must be modified as its prime star moves into that dutiful and more feminine *sign*.

In similar manner, though converse, to that forward shift of a single star, the movement of the *signs* through the *constellations* in a retrograde direction modifies their meanings for us at different periods in history. So, for example, when the *signs* and *constellations* were perfectly matched, *ARIES* to *ARIES*, and so on, each manifested in a very simple manner that was little influenced, if at all, by its neighbours; people simply behaved aggressively, or passively, or idly or industriously, according to their intrinsic natures, and without ulterior motives, much as the lower animals do.

But earlier, when the *sign Aries* was in *constellation Taurus*, humanity was chiefly engaged in the great struggle to reclaim and resettle the terrain of Earth after the mighty disaster that had afflicted it, as we shall see when we discuss *Taurus* in Chapter 6. And since *sign Aries* has shifted into *constellation Pisces* our aggression towards each other has veered more and more into the field of ideological and religious conflict.

The key to understanding this interrelationship of *sign* and *constellation* lies, then, with the location at any one time of the *Vernal Equinox*, Zero Degrees of *sign Aries*. In large measure, the interactions elsewhere will take their cues from this primary feature of order, the *sign* seeming to say to the *constellation* it has invaded: 'We must take note that *Aries* is in - - - - - (*Pisces, Aquarius*, whatever) and work together accordingly.' While star Regulus moves indeed into workaday *Virgo* by forward motion, that *sign* itself moves further into *Leo* and seeks greater dignity for human labour, while *sign Leo* itself shifts more into *Cancer* and expresses its august qualities of kingship with more feeling for the needs of its state or empire as a homeland of people.

In the rest of this volume we shall be careful to make clear when we are talking of *constellations*, and when of *(signs)*. And that seems a good way to do so:

When we say **Aries** we mean the *constellation*.
And by **(Aries)** we mean the *sign*.

And as we come to each Constellation (for we shall proceed in that manner) we shall do our best to remind the reader of this manner of distinction.

CHAPTER 4

How Stars are Classified

Astronomers have to have some means of identifying stars so that they can say what kind of star they are describing: old or young, very hot or comparatively cool, easily visible or needing a powerful telescope, and much more information about it, in such a way that each knows what another is saying.

We do not need to go into all their complex conventions here, but it will help if we understand and can use a little of them: first of all, we can talk about a star's brightness in the sky, as we see it, or what the astronomer calls its *Visual Magnitude*.

If all stars were the same distance from us, their (Visual) *Magnitude* would be the same as their (True) *luminosity*, but, in fact, they vary enormously in distance from us, measured usually in *light-years*, one light-year being the distance light travels in one of our years. The farther a star is from us, the less do we see of its true luminosity. For example, *Vega*, in the constellation of Lyra, appears just a little brighter than *Rigel*, in Orion, yet, in fact, Rigel is 961 times more luminous than Vega (and 50,000 more than our Sun). But Vega is only 26 light-years from us, whereas Rigel is 900 light-years distant. Luminosity is commonly expressed by a simple number indicating how many times brighter than our Sun the star really is.

The *Absolute Magnitude* of any star is what its Apparent (or

Visual) Magnitude would be if the star were 32.6 Lt-yrs (or 10 PARSECS) from us, and thus indicates the comparative True Luminosities of all stars. When the single word 'Magnitude' is used in most popular books on astronomy or astrology, it is normally meaning the Apparent, or Visual. This is also expressed by a number, such that 1 (one) is the mean of the Vis. Mags of a certain twenty bright stars, chosen by an agreement in 1850. If a star is brighter than that mean, it receives a minus rating (*Sirius* = −1.4; *Sun* = −26.7!); if less bright it gets a plus rating. *Vega*, one of the twenty, is rated at 0.0; *Rigel*, another of the twenty, is at 0.1; *Manubrium*, in Sagittarius, is at 4.5 and is only just visible to the naked eye, if you have good sight.

The use of Greek code letters, prefixed to the Latin genitive of a constellation's name, tells us that α is visually the brightest one in that constellation, β the second brightest, γ the third, and so on down the Greek alphabet, printed at the end of this chapter.

Some readers may like to know about *Spectral Class*, important to all astronomers but used by some astrologers also. A spectroscope uses a prism to break up ordinary white light into the seven colours of the visible spectrum, familiar to us all as a rainbow when water droplets in the air do the same job as a prism.

The light from a star can be broken up in the same way, but not all with the even spread of seven colours we get from white light. At various points the band of the spectrum will be crossed by thin black lines called 'Absorption Lines' which tell the astro-physicist, by the particular colours they cross and how close they are to each other, what chemical elements are present in the star, and which of them are predominant there. Moreover, the extent to which these lines are seen to be shifted *en bloc* to one or other end of the spectrum will tell us whether the star is approaching us (shift to the violet end), or receding from us (shift towards red), and how fast in either case. A further important bonus from the discovery of Absorption Lines was the confirmation that the 90 to 100 chemical elements familiar to us on Earth are also those which make up the rest of the Universe.

The basic spectral classification is shown by one of ten capital letters of the Latin alphabet in this order: W.O.B.A.F.G.K.M.R.N.S., where W denotes the hottest stars, S the coolest and most nearly solid. Contrary to popular belief, they are not just huge balls of hydrogen; the hottest are very rich in helium, while our local Sun, a G class, is notably rich in calcium along with hydrogen, a situation not unlike ourselves. An easy, even though slightly childish way to remember the letters in order is the mnemonic:

Wow! Oh Be a Fine Girl, Kiss Me right Now, Sweetie.

The Wow is often left out, W stars being very few in number, but a further refinement is obtained by subdividing each letter group into ten numerical classes, 0 to 9. So a G0 star is not very different to an F, while a G9 is almost a K. And a further subdivision is made by using one of seven Roman numerals next (I to VII) to denote the luminosity of the star: I = Supergiant (very bright); II = Bright Giant; III = Giant; IV = sub-Giant; V = main sequence (i.e. most common) dwarfs; VI = sub-dwarfs; VII = white dwarfs.

Lastly there may be appended a Latin letter in small case, giving details about the particular lines seen in the spectrum: 'emission'(e), 'nebulous'(n), 'sharp'(s), 'interstellar'(k), 'metallic'(m), 'peculiar'(p), and 'variable'(v). So, for example, our Sun is a G2V, *Algol* is a B8V. *Stella Mira* varies from M5 to M9e.

In all of that technicality, perhaps the most relevant feature for us is how intimately Men have come to know their celestial companions, and what joy even the most materialist astronomer among us feels as he talks of them as he would of his living human friends. Whether or not he consciously shares the present author's philosophy, he is a leader of mankind towards a greater kinship with the Infinity of which we are an integral part, an Infinity which is also the Divinity.

And now, the Greek Alphabet:

α	=	alpha	ν	=	nu
β	=	beta	ξ	=	xi
γ	=	gamma	ο	=	omicron
δ	=	delta	π	=	pi
ϵ	=	epsilon	ρ	=	rho
ζ	=	zeta	σ	=	sigma
η	=	eta	τ	=	tau
θ	=	theta	υ	=	upsilon
ι	=	iota	ϕ	=	phi
κ	=	kappa	χ	=	chi
λ	=	lambda	ψ	=	psi
μ	=	mu	ω	=	omega

CHAPTER 5

Aries the Ram

One of the earliest constellations to have been recognised, this is also **(Aries),** the first sign of the Zodiac, marker by its cusp (that is, 0 degrees of the Sign) of the Vernal Equinox:- The day in Spring on which daylight and darkness are each twelve hours in length. The date of this event is March 21st (20th in leap years), and, of course, it is Spring only in Earth's northern hemisphere. Of all the animals to be seen prancing on our Easter Cards, the lamb is surely the one most popular, though, of course, many other animals also have young at this time, and the root of the lamb's popularity is astrological. **Aries** is just as much a lamb as a ram.

This astrological theme is seen in religion too. Christian litany is full of references to Jesus as The Lamb (of God), and the foundation of Christianity is commonly said to have coincided with the start of the 'Piscean Age', when the cusp **Aries**, the Sign, moved out of that Constellation into its preceding neighbour **Pisces**. As has been noted in the previous chapter, this did not in fact happen until the year

217 A.D., but then the new religion likewise took three hundred years to become established, in 325 A.D.. So the conicidence of the two can be said to be accurate enough.

Other commentators have seen astrological significance in the story of the near-sacrifice of Isaac by the patriarch Abraham, which ended with the father being directed instead to sacrifice a *ram* Divinely caught in a nearby thicket. Isaac had a half-brother, Ishmail, so the story is reminiscent of the many myths of one of two brothers being scarificed for the benefit of the other: Cain & Abel, Castor & Pollux, and so-on. The suggestion here is that the Isaac incident marks the end of the Gemini era of 'twin sacrifice', the shifting of the Vernal Equinox into Taurus, the Constellation and Sign most associated with the culture that began with Abraham, and a looking forward to the Aries era yet to come, when the culture which the patriarch was just initiating would burst forth to conquer all around it, remembering as we should how Aries is considered ruled by Mars the planet of war and conquest. We may also note that the name Abraham or Abrahm, means 'Servant of the Divinity' or, in its form Ibrahim, 'Servant of the Merciful One', in the culture which derives its descent through Ishmail especially.

Aries is poor in prominent stars, and is hardly noticeable with the naked eye in less than a perfectly clear sky without moonlight. Just three of its stars, α Arietis, *Hamal*, then β, *Sharatan,* and γ, *Mesartim,* figure in astrology.

Hamal, or *Ar Ras Al Hamal*, to use its full title, means The Head of the (male) sheep, and this characterizes well its meaning astrologically. The famous astronomer-astrologer Ptolemy devised planetary analogues for many stars, so that he said *Hamal* has the qualities of Mars and Saturn together, Mars the more dominant. It is a good description of people with this star strong in their horoscopes – headstrong and often aggressive, yet potentially capable leaders and protectors of their community, all the qualities of a ram.

Sharatan, from Al *Sharat,* The Sign, was the marker of the Vernal Equinox at the date it was so named, so that is what is 'signed'. In Ptolemy's list, it is another Mars-Saturn type, and it does indeed show similar qualites in people to those of *Hamal*.

Mesartim, γ Arietis, is a word meaning Ministers (in old Hebrew) and it is noteworthy that Ptolemy gives this near neighbour of the other two the same planetary simile in the opposite order: Saturn-Mars. Our astrology here must take on pin-point accuracy but the implication is that *Mesartim* shows up more of the protective-administrative quality, less of the impulsive aggressiveness of *Hamal* and *Sharatan*.

All three of these **Aries** stars have been in the Sign **(Taurus)** for about 200 or 300 years now, *Hamal* just over 600 in fact, and in this same period we have seen large-scale aggression change its nature from the barbaric raiding and migrations of earlier centuries to the building of large empires which had to be administered and kept in peace and good order, as well as exploited by their conquerors. This is all typical both of the Sign **(Taurus)** and of the planet Saturn.

CHAPTER 6

Taurus the Bull

This, the second of the Zodiac Signs, and as ancient in human history as the first, is the primary 'earth' Sign, contrasting with Aries's 'fire' quality, and thus marks mankind's early steps in establishing settled communities on selected agricultural land, after the nomadic wanderings that were his lot during the recovery from The Disaster. We could call it his convalescent and occupational-therapy period.

The Constellation **Taurus**, much of it now in the Sign **(Gemini),** is a large one, rich in major stars, including the mighty Red Giant we call variously *Oculus Tauri,* 'Eye of the Bull', or *Aldebaran,* from the Arabic for 'The Follower'.

Many stories are told about this famed Bull. The god Jupiter (Zeus) was surely the archetype of Don Giovanni in amorous adventuring, and on one occasion set his heart on Europa, daughter of the Cretan king Agenor.

Failing to gain her hand by consent of the lady or her father, Zeus took on the form of a white bull, persuaded her to try a ride on him and promptly swam away to sea with her. Within the sheer fun of the tale is a note of the astrological quality of the two planets which have 'dignity' in **(Taurus)**: Venus which rules it, Moon exalted there. Venus is noted there both for its artistry – (a bull that can induce anyone to ride it must surely be a beauty) – and for its forthright pursuit of romance, lacking the negotiating skill of the other Sign it rules, **(Libra)**; Moon in **(Taurus)** is noted for a very genuine love quality, but highly possessive with it.

Myth and legend abound with references to this animal all over the world, it having been sacred in the Middle East and Africa, and still so in India; oxen were probably tamed for service to man sooner than the horse. It was sacred in Egypt, there associated with the god-man Osiris who taught civilisation and farming there, and it is also the Minotaur of the Minoan (Cretan) Empire. The slaying of this bull by the hero Hercules doubtless describes the conflict between Greece and Crete, ending in 1754 BC with the destruction of Minoan life by the volcanic explosion of Thera.

Mithraic culture in the Euphrates area (Iraq) also revered the bull and Judaic culture tells how Moses fought against bull worship, (the golden calf), among his tribes after the Exodus from Egypt. Babylon and Persia had their bull demi-gods too. During much of the earlier times of those cultures, the Vernal Equinox was in **Taurus**, so taking and cultivating land was the major human task.

The prime star of Taurus, as already noted, is *Oculus Tauri* (α) or *Aldebaran* as it is better known now. This is one of the four key stars in the heavens, also called Archangel Stars, Michael in this case – military commander of the Heavenly Host. It is also called 'Watcher of the East', possibly since it is the bull's eye, though each of the Archangels is a 'Watcher of'; Gabriel *(Fomalhaut)* of the South, Raphael *(Regulus)* of the North, Oriel *(Antares)* of the West. At one time they marked the two Equinoxes and the two Solstices.

To Ptolemy *Aldebaran* was a Mars-type star, and indeed the red giant can be mistaken for that red planet at times, so it is no surprise that it has been much associated with war and military careers, and 'The Follower', as its name translates, can well be taken to imply following in the steps of the celestial general, Michael. The idea put forward by some mundane-minded astronomers, that the name means only that the star comes soon after the The Pleiades star group, makes little sense since every star follows some other in that manner. In astrological practice, it is not assumed that *Aldebaran* necessarily promises *success* in war – unless it is especially well aspected to other items on the horoscope, as opposite to it is the Mars-Jupiter star *Antares* (q.v. in Scorpio), for the inclusion of Jupiter in the Ptolemaic styling of this star actually implies more power than in *Aldebaran*. Any general launching an attack with one of the pair in the Ascendant for himself should remember that the other fellow has the other star in HIS Ascendant. Many generals have discounted this even after consulting an astrologer! (And have regretted it).

Aldebaran has been in the sign **(Gemini)** since 1286 AD, just around the height of the Christian Crusades against Islam, an interesting indicator of conflict between two world schools of thought. *Antares*, for the other side in the conflict, went into religious Sagittarius in 1272 AD and showed its superiority, perhaps, since the Crusaders never did dislodge the Saracens.

Al Nath, β Tauri, second brightest in the Constellation, has the same Mars quality according to Ptolemy, but lacks the august Archangelic status of *Aldebaran*. The name means 'The One Who Butts (or Gores)', deriving from its position on one of the bull's horn-tips. So it is more of the officer in the front line than the general at G.H.Q. if we stay with the military scene or, since Mars is not only the planet of war but also of surgery, engineering, iron and steel generally, *Al Nath* will show up practical skill in any of these professions. Some astronomers have considered *Al Nath* to be in the neighbouring Constellaiton, *Auriga* (q.v) where it is γ, third brightest, under the name Al Ka'b or Al Aqib, The Heel of the Reinholder. Either way it has been in the Sign **(Gemini)** since 362 AD.

The Hyades

This small group of six stars, including the Eye of Taurus, is often given the status of a mini Constellation itself. Greek mythology saw them as the daughters of Atlas and Aethra, major figures in the pre-disaster period of our history, and somehow counted seven of them where we find only six. The girls' names are variously given in the works of the Greeks: Kleea, Eudora, Koronis, Phaeo, Phaesula and two more which you may choose from Ambrosia, Dione and Thyene. Like their half-sisters *The Pleiades* (q.v.), they were a sorrowful group – understandably after seeing Father try in vain to keep the sky (i.e.; Phaeton's debris) up off the Earth – and they have long portended rain, to both farmers and seafarers. Apart from the special meaning accorded to *Aldebaran*, not now counted as one of the group, only two are as worthy of our note: γ Tauri, *Prima Hyadum*, and ϵ *Ain Hyadum*. *Prima Hyadum*, less commonly *Awwal Aldabarin* (First of the Followers), is a Saturn-Mercury star in Ptolemy's coding, which we might well describe as unhappy thoughts, and so it shows up when the star is on a difficult spot or planet in an horoscope. But if it be harmonious in aspect, instead, the same star denotes a good clear thinker, writer and speaker.

Ain Hyadum, given a Mercury-Mars rating by Ptolemy, may be counted a yet stronger symbol of communicative ability than *Prima*. The name *Ain* itself recalls that exalted level above the Qabalah's 'Tree of Life', only two steps down from the Godhead, entirely appropriate for a star so close to the Archangel signified by *Aldebaran* that it is more an additional quality to the greater star than a symbol in its own right. We must suppose that good communicative ability, the quality of Mercury, is an essential for a good general or any other commander of a large community in action.

Of the Hyades overall, we can now add the note that these princesses of one of Earth's most powerful rulers in the run-up to the Disaster would indeed have been among those required to communicate the news to a panic-stricken population and to exercise firm control on them. And that is very much the quality we find in this part of **Taurus**, now in the second decanate (5 to 10°) of **(Gemini)**.

The Pleiades

Although we dealt with the Hyades first, because they surround the chief star of Taurus, the Pleiades are in fact some 10° earlier in the Constellation, rather higher in the sky, and are still just in the last degree of the Sign (**Taurus**). It is doubtful if any other small star group has had so much written about it as have the famed 'Seven Sisters'. A district of London has been named in their honour – and an ale house there too! Not one culture anywhere on Earth has failed to make an important celestial station of them, and always with feminine connotation.

To the Persians they were effectively the beginning of their Zodiac and called Parwiin, as we read from Omar Khayyam:

> 'I tell you this: When starting from the Goal,
> Over the shoulders of the Flaming Foal
> Of Heaven, Parwiin and Mushtara they flung,
> In my predestined plot of Dust and Soul ...'

In ancient China they were the Seven Sisters of Industry, a title that Chairman Mao well could have coined in our own century! Young ladies of ancient China worshipped them in a fertility rite, not at all what the Chairman would approve of, though ironically the group was actually called *Mao* by their ancient worshippers!

The precise origin of their Greek title, by which we know them now, is obscure. The verb 'πλειν', to sail, has been suggested since Greek mariners took the rising of the group to mark the arrival of good voyaging weather. Others have rejected this 'modern' derivation in favour of 'πλειws', 'many', akin to their Arabic title, A1 Thurayya. Several Greek poets called them 'πελειαδες' – Rock Doves. (Our times are not the first to use 'birds' to mean female humanity!). In their accounts, these seven daughters of King Atlas by his first wife, and thus half-sisters of the Hyades, were transmuted into doves as the result of their grief for their father's vain labours but, being wingless, were generously placed in the heavens by the Divinity. We may well wonder what actual fate during the catastrophe the myth is trying to describe.

Only one of the Pleiades is commonly known by name: *Alcyone*, η Tauri. This is actually the name of the Atlantaean nymph, queen to Poseidon and mother of the later king Hyrieus, though that may not account for the use of the same name given to the star. We also repeat names in successive generations of a family. More probably, this one was a leading figure to her thirteen sisters and half-sisters. In other cultures, other names have been given, such as the Arabic Al Na'ir, 'The Bright One', or Al Wasat, 'The Middle One'. The contention that the more familiar name is connected with Halcyon, kingfisher, is the cause of much dispute among 'learned men', though there is no good reason why such a beautiful star should not have been named after a very beautiful bird – or vice-versa.

Alcyone, and the whole Pleiades group, is noted in astrology for its association with deep sorrows and tragedies, bereavements showing strongly with this star. Its position by longitude soon after *Algol* in Perseus (q.v.) may account for this gloomy quality, since *Algol* is so much connotated with violent death in mundane astrology, and that of course means bereavement for someone else. As a practising astrological consultant, however, the present author has found that one or both of these stars prominent, even though 'afflicted', on one's horoscope makes for an excellent counsellor to others in the time of bereavement, with a special gift for bringing out the brighter spiritual significance of Death as the transition to Greater Life and this so very often relieves the counsellor him or herself from the misery that others so commonly suffer in that area of life.

And now we return to the main body of TAURUS

Al Hecka, ζ Tauri, marks the tip of the bull's southern horn and, as we might expect for this piece of weaponry, Ptolemy classed it as a Mars star. Tracing the Arabic original of the name is not easy, early western scholars having generally made a poor job of that language. It may drive from *Al Qarn*, The Horn, a difficult near-K sound for us to pronounce, but more closely it resembles *Al Haikal* which can men either a Huge Beast (such as a bull) or a Temple. To the Chinese it was Tien Gwan, the Heavenly Gate, so the Arabic 'Temple' is at least as likely as Huge Beast. One further possible Arabic origin is from *Al Hak'ah*, the White Spot (on the horn tip).

Astrologically it is counted an unfortunate star but, even if we may believe in 'goodies and baddies', it is risky to blame only *Al Hecka* here, since four other stars lie within two degrees of it – *Mintaka*, *Al Nath*, *Ensis (Hatysa*, *Na'ir*), and *Al Nilam*. All five stars, currently around 22° of (**Gemini**), mark a combative nature with the tongue, and sometimes manually too, which can indeed lead to misfortune, although the victim may well be convinced that it is 'all for the cause', and that the 'reward in Heaven' will compensate for the suffering here below. So again, both the bull's horn and the temple or gate of heaven seem appropriate symbols for this bright star.

CHAPTER 7

Gemini the Twins

Gemini is one of the few constellations which the author finds both easy to locate in the sky, and easy to recognise as what its name proclaims it to be. It really does look like a pair of the artist Lowry's famous 'matchstick people', though they have to share three legs between the two of them. He would doubtless have been moved by this symbol of the poverty among the Lancashire people dear in his heart.

It is the first of the 'Air Signs' in the Zodiac, denoting the use of the human faculties of thought, speech and enquiry, and thus it is appropriately the first 'Human Sign,' the others being (**Virgo**) (**Sagittarius**) and (**Aquarius**).

Both as a Constellation and a Sign, however, it is far from being the symbol of light-hearted superficiality which cheap astrology makes of it. In the history of our recovery from the Phaeton disaster, the entry of the Vernal Equinox into **Gemini** was about 2,000 years after the event, just about when humanity was venturing cautiously around its haven localities to find out if it was safe to come out yet. The same is still characteristic of 'Geminis' (people born with Sun in that Sign); they are curious about everything but cautious of going too far – a caution which 'deeper' types mistake for lack of desire to know – and they easily become excited by politics, the rivalry between parties and factions, the mutual threatening between nations and the overall threat which all that implies for human survival.

Ancient legend and myth abound in stories of mortal combat between twins, Cain & Abel, Castor & Pollux, being only two such pairs made familiar to us from Hebrew and Greek sources. More abstractly, the Chinese came to regard Gemini as symbolic of Yin and Yang, and some cultures have seen them as pairs of humans or animals without the added idea of conflict between them. These are very much a minority, however, and still fewer are cultures seeing only a single creature in this Constellation. The necessary death of one twin must have its roots in the near impossibility of raising two offspring at once in dire circumstances, and the practice of eliminating one has still not ceased in some poor and primitive communities to this day.

The Cain & Abel story is especially interesting since the victor there was the grower of crops, slaying the keeper of animals. We may see in this the advance of human food production, from the nomadic life driving herds to the settlement of territory and the improvement of land through human skill, a campaign still being waged today. Why this so offended a 'Lord God' is a matter of conjecture still: The suggestion that this particular 'lord' was less than Divine, and was really some mortal personage of political power, who favoured the old ways, has been voiced by many before now, and seems as feasible at least as any moral, ethical or theological explanation for that grim period in history.

Because of its clarity in the sky, no less than seven of **Gemini's** stars have found usage by astrologers: In zodiacal order they are Tejat Prior, Dirah (or Nuhaiti), Al Hena, Al Wasat, Propus, Castor, and Pollux. All lie today between 3 and 23° of the Sign **(Cancer).** As with the other Constellations, however, we shall take these stars in order of Visual Magnitude, symbolic of their importance to us.

Castor, then, α Geminorum, is our first subject, and an interesting one it surely is. He was the horseman of the twins, just as Abel was the animal keeper, and he shared Abel's fate of being slain by his brother. Pollux got his brother drunk to make the task easier, or as one wag among classical scholars put it: He got Castor oiled! In astrology, generally, *Castor* is counted a star of misfortune, and the specific association with breaking an arm or leg may come from the Ptolemaic classification of this as a Mercury star; that planet is much associated with the arms, or the limbs generally. *Castor* is also noted in natal astrology for proneness to nervous breakdowns, and the author has often found it prominent on the horoscopes of his many clients in neurotic distress.

But *Castor's* Mercury quality does have a better side to it, as does all else counted 'bad' in this world of the heavens. People with it prominent and well aspected are exceptionally gifted intellectually, a good creative quality along with this – a bonus from the combination of intellectual **Gemini** constellation and intuitive Sign **(Cancer)**. Where these potential geniuses often need help is in not letting their concern for others go 'over the top' beyond their own sensible state of responsibility and practical ability to help, the negative side of the combined **Gemini-(Cancer)** qualities. *Castor's* connection with Mercury goes deeper yet. The Greeks knew it at one time as *Apollo*, and, at another time, they called the planet Mercury by that name. Still earlier, *Apollo* was that other sun which we have since called *Phaeton*, which is no more. And just as that was Sun's close companion then, so is Mercury its closest one now. And to cap that, *Castor*, the former *Apollo*, is in fact a Binary Pair of stars, as once were Sun and Phaeton. As we have remarked already, a binary pair evokes a deep-seated fear in humanity, an unconscious recall of The Disaster, so that we tend to react to it just as one does all the wrong things in a moment of crisis, if it happens to half-awaken in one some earlier trauma of the same kind. The author has experimented with acquainting 'Castor-stricken' clients with the true story behind our fear of binaries, and the results so far in banishing panic reactions in crises have been very heartening.

Pollux, β Geminorum, is by Ptolemy's account a Mars star, appropriate for the twin who killed the other; he was also the immortal one, a son of Zeus (Jupiter) and thus favoured by him, an interesting contrast to Jehovah's (Jupiter's) anger at Cain's behaviour. At certain periods, this star has also been called *Hercules*, not to be confused with the Constellation of the same name, the hero of so many labours and deeds of valour in humanity's growth. While often tarred with the same brush as *Castor* in some astrology, it is generally counted a more positive symbol and the underlying reason may be that it is close in spectral class and colour to the Sun, and, though having at least five faint companions as seen from Earth, these are in fact far distant beyond it: It is not a Binary. Prominent on a horoscope, it certainly can show aptitude for getting into quarrels, but in a well configured situation it also denotes a power of penetration on the mental plane, aided no doubt by its near neighbour in longitude, the Mercury-Mars star *Procyon,* α Canis Minoris, discussed later.

Al Hena, γ Geminorum, is our next subject. A better rendering of the Arabic is *Al Han'ah*, an identifying mark on a horse or camel, made with tar-paint. An earlier name was Almeisan – one who marches proudly – but this was apparently dropped as several stars carried the same name. Nonetheless, it seems right for a prominent star in the feet of the Twins. Popular astrology has associated this star especially with accidents to the feet, loving to make the worst of every star it can blame for something or other, but it seems quite unnecessary to use *Al Hena* for this purpose, since right opposite to it in the Zodiac is *Facies*, equally associated with accidents – and with more reason, since Ptolemy rates it a Sun-Mars type whereas *Al Hena* is a more peaceable Mercury-Venus. We should perhaps have remarked sooner that in astrology a star is found to show its influence both at its own location and right opposite to it. (See Sagittarius for Facies).

From a combination of *Al Hena's* placing in its Constellation and in Sign, **(Cancer)**, and the Ptolemaic simile for it, it is not hard to guess that this star should show up our artistic skills, especially with the written and spoken word, and our abilities to negotiate a peaceful solution to disputes among people. And so indeed it does. We get to the roots of problems and move matters forward from there, and gaining 'identity', distinction, that is, for our efforts.

Al Hena is one of Pollux's feet, and almost on the same longitude is *Mebsuta,* or *Mobsuta,* ε Geminorum, on Castor's knee. This star is not a regular with astrologers but its name means 'well', or 'O.K.', an additional confirmation of the positive qualities of *Al Hena.*

Al Wasat, δ Geminorum, is in the waist area of the Twins, the name meaning just that: the Middle. Ptolemy makes a Saturn type of it, so we should expect serious meaning here. It is well within the orb of influence of *Castor*, and vice-versa, and so adds its Saturnine weight to that star, helping to account for the heaviness and tendency to pessimism found in people with 18 – 20° of **(Cancer)** active in their charts. Apart from that, however, *Al Wasat* does show up a quality of being able to speak with clear authority when others are waffling, and prominence in public affairs or management is often the result.

Tejat Prior, η Geminorum, has a hybrid Arabic-Latin name meaning the Underneath Front (star). Within two degrees of it on Castor's foot is *Tejat Posterior,* μ Gem., the Underneath Rear star, naturally. By the bye, *Tahat* is a better pronunciation. *Posterior* also goes by the names *Dirah* and *Nuhaitai.* Neither of those relates to Gemini as we know it, the first being either a breastplate mis-spelt or an arm just as mis-spelt, while Nuhaitai is a pair of camel humps. People do make 'unofficial' constellations at times, one popular lecturer at Greenwich having made a coathanger from Leo and a bit more, and a third bear elsewhere to complete the kiddies' story with Ursa Major and Ursa Minor!

Both *Tejats* or *Tahats* are Mercury-Venus stars by Ptolemy: thus again, we find that quality which we saw in *Al*

Hena, the ability to express ideas in reasonable and acceptable ways which win because of their manifest intelligence. Some commentators have, as usual when they mention almost any star, drawn attention to the capacity found in these three to capitalise on the popularity one may gain from the ease of the 'public appeal' quality latent in them, and to use it for unscrupulous ends. But it is doubtful if there is any advantage at all in human affairs which may not be abused, if one is so minded, so why single out this one for special condemnation?!

All three stars, the two *Tejats* and *Al Hena,* fill the first 10°, or Decanate, of the Cardinal Sign **(Cancer)**, into which they entered in 1349, 1621 and 1755 A.D. respectively. Each of these dates, within a year or two, was significant in the rise of European thought and literature from the Renaissance onwards.

Propus, ι Geminorum, is the last of the significant stars in Gemini, its position being just over one degree short of *Castor*, and it is yet another Mercury-Venus type. A good deal of confusion surrounds this name in various old astronomical works, some of which derive it from the Greek **προποϵ** and apply it to *Tejat Prior* in Castor's foot. But it is now quite definitely the star between the twins' shoulders, where they come 'close' together, as the word implies in Latin. So we should read into this star the qualities of co-operation, of 'two heads being better than one' and of associative thinking – just as we are doing right now, along with those now-familiar Mercury-Venus attributes we have been seeing already. The associative-thinking quality is very vital in the practice of astrology when it comes to reading an horoscope, and so naturally *Propus* in a good placing on a natal chart tells us we have a good astrologer born there. But in psychotherapy we know too that associative thinking is a feature of such pathological states as paranoia, where quite unconnected and innocent actions by other people may be welded by a patient into a thrilling plot of conspiracy against him or her.

So *Propus*, with the 'help' of nearby saturnine *Al Wasat*, may be yet another factor in the negative, 'nervous breakdown' qualities which we note to occur sometimes with *Castor.* Apart from drawing attention of the patient to the ancient historic reasons for our unconscious states of fear (for which refer again to *Castor*), a good therapy for sufferers from *Propus* in particular is to encourage them to employ their associative-thinking capacities deliberately and usefully, so that they become skilled in the control of them. A good astrologer is preferable to a sick paranoiac any time!

There are plenty more stars in Gemini, one of the richest of all in easily visible stars, but the rest are, for our purposes, only the 'extras' among the 'stars' in this rich piece of celestial theatre.

CHAPTER 8

Cancer the Crab

Cancer is the next Ecliptic Constellation after **Gemini**, and not one of the outstandingly visible ones, though easy enough to find on a clear moonless night, resembling a large X with a small triangle at its intersection. As a Zodiacal Sign **(Cancer)** is the fourth one, the second of Cardinal quality, the first of the Water Element. Its ruler is the Moon. In mythology, it is the Crab which attempted to aid *Hydra*, the Water Snake, in its combat with *Hercules*; and the giant trod on **Cancer**, to the cost of its life. The goddess Juno, queen to Jupiter, did not favour Hercules anyway, so she rescued (the soul of) Cancer and placed it in the heavens.

Make what you will of the charming story as a fairytale, it has much interest symbolically and psychologically. The crab is not at all the strong creature it appears to be, for many other predators find it easy to avoid the menace of the claws and to attack beneath the tough shell, where the crab is, to coin a pun, 'easy meat'. And that combination of tough, even menacing demeanour to cover a really rather vulnerable self within is a common feature of 'Cancerians'. They are easily persuaded to join in battles for which they are not adequate, being unwilling to suffer the loss of face which refusal may bring in the eyes of their companions. They are great home-lovers, as all the books say about them, analogising the need for a roof over their heads with the crab's need of a shell on its back. And the role of the mother goddess, Juno in the story, shows up well the need which these people manifest to mother or to be mothered.

We can take the symbolism deeper yet. From the works of Otto Muck and others, Sun would seem to have been in *Cancer* at the time of the Disaster that showed up the vulnerability of us all to forces we had had no reason to suspect: and the near loss of our home planet, our reproductive capacity and our emotional stability are enough to give **Cancer**, and **(Cancer)**, all the qualities just noted, plus the emotional extremes for which it is also known. The arrival of Moon, Luna, upon the scene at the same time makes that a highly suitable ruler of **(Cancer)**, and quite apart from its unquestionable physical effects upon our nervous systems.

And now we can have a look at the stars of **Cancer**, all of which are currently in the Sign **(Leo)**. The brightest star in the constellation is β Cancri, not α; so either their relative magnitudes have changed over two centuries or else the astronomer got it wrong. In point of fact, δ and ι are also a little brighter than α. It is surprising that neither ι nor B has been figured in astrology, perhaps confirming that they have only reached their present magnitudes in fairly recent times. In the case of ι, it is not too important since its zodiacal longitude is close to that of North Asellus. γ Cancri.

For astrologers who want to include β, the brightest in **Cancer**, its name is *Al Tarf*, 'The End', meaning only that it is on the tip of the southern hind leg of the Crab. It is an Orange Giant star, 170 light years distant from us. The Zodiacal longitude lies between 0° and 1° **(Leo)**. We have no recorded planetary simile from Ptolemy, presumably since he did not use it, but the colour is of a spectral class in the

K/M region, like *Aldebaran, Pollux* or *Antares*, and so a Mars simile would be appropriate.

The tip of the forward southern leg is *Acubens*, α Cancri, familiar in astrology as a Saturn-Mercury type, thus more cautious than the martian quality of β, though the piercing or stinging notion in the Latin form of the name still contains the note of attack. (The Crab, Lobster and the Scorpion were once all thought to have stings, from their somewhat similar appearances). It is also suggested, however, that the name originates from the Arabic *Al Zubanah*, The Claw, and indeed this star does represent the southern of the crab's claws. We shall find later that several more Saturn-Mercury stars are on the points of various weaponry carried by the characters in the heavens.

So one significance of *Acubens* is the enforced use of applied intelligence when finding oneself in combat at someone else's behest, as we may say the Crab's front leg finds itself driven on by the Mars *Al Tarf* on the back leg. But a generally more positive quality to read from *Acubens* is that of a sharp intellect and ease of coming to grips with problems, for which one may earn quite high public renown. But, again, there is the note of doing this under the pressure of others demanding 'from behind'.

At the centre of **Cancer** is a small triangle formed by the stars *North Asellus* (γ), *South Asellus* (δ), and *Praesepe* (M44). And these are the three remaining important stars in the Constellation for us to consider.

Asellus is Latin for Donkey, and the 'North' and 'South' are often printed as *Asellus Borealis* and *Asellus Australis* respectively, and also they may be given in atrocious transliterations of their names in Arabic: (North) *Himar El Schemali*, (South) *Himar El Genubi*. It may not be any better to see *Al Himar As Shamalii* and *Al Himar Al Janubi* but we have now covered all likelihoods. The pair together may be called 'The Aselli' or 'The Hamir', or Himarain'.

Their names arise from a more pastoral than astronomical or astrological appellation given them by early Greeks and Arabs alike, but we find that this has worked its way into astrology just as much as the positions they hold in **Cancer**. And so they are a mini-constellation in their own right. They are so close together in longitude that they may usually be considered as one unit.

The 'patient donkey' is a lovable creature, agreed, but it can be very self-willed and unco-operative indeed at times of its own choosing. And the *Aselli* reflect this to near perfection. They display all the moodiness of **Cancer** at its most negative, while in **(Leo)**, where they have resided since 1472 AD (North) and 1397 AD (South), they can put up a wonderful display of stubbornness and impatience at one and the same time. Both are Mars-Sun stars by Ptolemy, and one can marvel at the utter frustration one suffers in trying to persuade or even just help someone with their own Sun or Mars (or both!!!) of these stars. Mars-Sun stars, along with Mars-Moon and the reverses of both combinations, are generally known as 'blind stars', indicative of eyesight problems, and astrologers sometimes warn clients to avoid any surgery on or near the eyes when such stars are activated by the transit of a significant planet (for that particular horoscope) over them. It is often well to take such advice too, just as one can often say with confidence that one of these stars on the cusp of a sixth house (that of physical health) reveals a basic tendency to eyesight troubles.

But 'blind stars' have another, far more positive quality, which is of at least as much importance if the astrologer is trying to help the client to actualise the full potential which the horoscope shows to be there. These stars show up an ability to 'see' what other folks cannot. If the Sun be on such a star, and favourably aspected, there will be that intuitive sense which makes one 'see the possibilities' where others miss them, and this is very much the case with these two *Aselli* in **(Leo)**, a Sign so much associated with leadership in all the fields of human affairs, business, politics, religious office etc. A conjunction with Moon, Mercury, Venus or Neptune, again well aspected, takes that intuition deeper and will often reveal the poet, painter, musician unusually gifted, composer, psychic 'medium' or astrologer. In all these cases, too, there is that patience for which the Donkey is respected, a quality necessary for all really reliable psychism. Perhaps when the Donkey is being stubborn, he is seeing something in the path which his impatient master cannot or will not see.

Praesepe, or *Praesaepe*, is the last of the **Cancer** stars we need to say much about. It is not one star but a whole cluster of some 75 of them, at a mean distance of some 520 light years from us. It is easily seen on a good night, a faint misty patch about the size of the Pleiades. Since it is a cluster, it cannot be given the usual identification by the Spectral Class coding but it is number 44 in the catalogue of clusters and nebulae drawn up by the astronomer Messier, thus 'M44'. The name means 'a Stable' or a 'Pen' (for animals), and it may thus be considered the stable for the *Aselli*.

Praesepe is also commonly known today as the 'Beehive', on account of the cluster's shape and the swarm of bees implied by the large number of stars in it. The thought of those female insects with stings fits nicely with the Ptolemaic classification as a Mars-Moon star, even though he did not know of its beehive appearance. (To him it was a single faint star). One of the living wonders of the heavens is that so very often we receive meaning from them in ways which span whole centuries of time and may even be considered to transcend time per se.

The three stars, *Praesepe* and the *Aselli*, lie within 1° 29' overall, so that astrologically we must really take them as a single unit of their combined qualities: three parts of Mars, two of Sun and one of Moon in the celestial recipe book. *Praesepe*, then, adds the lunar ingredient, which we can define as (a) providing a home or base from which the *Aselli* operate and (b) giving a mundane effectiveness to the more remotely celestial qualities of the Donkeys. Anciently, the Moon was the home of the gods who visited and ruled Earth; today many astrologers see it as an 'amplifier' without which the influences of the other planets, 'real' or symbolic, would not be effective enough to make astrology work. So *Praesepe* may be seen as 'making the *Aselli* work'.

The busy atmosphere of the *Beehive* presents the same idea.

But the inclusion of a lunar quality with the others also emphasies that moody and unpredictable quality which we already saw from the siting of the *Aselli* in the Constellation of **Cancer**. It is this which gives *Praesepe* its bad name in old-fashioned astrology, and it is amusing to ponder the idea that terrestrial donkeys get their less endearing characteristics from the stable of their celestial archetypes!! But, more seriously, people with the three of these stars strong in their horoscopes, favourably aspected, do show a capacity for co-operation with others, the secret of much of their success in life, symbolised by both the regime of a Beehive and by a Stable that is the one home for two Donkeys.

CHAPTER 9

Leo the Lion

Leo has long been a popular favourite amoung both Constellations and Signs of the Zodiac. Although **(Cancer)** has contained Midsummer Day for centuries now,it is still **(Leo)**, ruled by the Sun and pictured very often as a stately lion, alert but at rest, which we feel to be most representative of the 'hazy lazy days of summer' when all seems well. It is also the Sign of Kings, Majesty and Lordship in general, and we all, save but the most dedicated (or dessicated) rebels, love the show which goes with all that, even if our part in it is only to cheer from the sidelines, wave a flag – and pay for it! We are all Lords in our hearts; a cursory study of linguistics shows that nearly all ethnic groups have names which imply lordship in them: Teuton, Frank, Arab, Gael, Celt, Latin and very many more.

(Leo) is also the Fifth Sign of the Zodiac, and thus symbolic of the Fifth House of the horoscope – the House of Joy and Love, of free flowing Inspiration and Creativity, of the blooming of the Arts. It is sometimes said to reveal the

Soul (of the horoscope's native), a fair observation since more precisely it shows up the works of the Inner Self in the outer world: 'By their works ye shall know them.'

The Constellation of **Leo** is large, easily seen, even in poor night conditions blurred by city lighting, and a truly splendid sight. Its prime star, *Regulus*, is bright enough to shine even through thin cloud layers. Six more of its stars are also easily visible, having magnitudes better than 4.

Regulus, α Leonis, has to be where we begin, though it lies nearer the middle than the beginning of the figure, taking the position of the Lion's heart. For this reason, it is also called *Cor Leonis*, the name common for it about the times of Shakespeare and William Lilly. Earlier it was *Rex*, the simple Latin for King, and Ptolemy knew it in Greek as Βασιλισκος (Basiliskos) of the same meaning. Some dispute exists as to who first called it *Regulus*, and why: Copernicus gets the credit usually, but while some say he named it after the famous Roman general of the First Punic War, others (this author included) think it more likely that it just sounded grander than *Rex*.

Every major culture has paid similar tribute to *Regulus*. In Babylon it was *Sharru*, the King; *Magha* (Mighty) in India. To Persians it was *Miyan* the Centre (of the Universe). To the pre-Islamic Arabs also it was *Malikyy*, Kingly, but the Muslim savant Al Biruni called it *Al Kalb Al Asad*, Heart of the Lion, and strongly linked some particular astronomical configuration, involving this star culminating over the Holy Province of Hijaz (Mecca and district) with the birth date of Islam.

Centuries earlier, the Akkadians gave it the very interesting title *Amil Gal Ur*, 'King of the Heavenly Sphere', acknowledging as their source for that title the Fifth Station of Antediluvian astronomy and/or astrology (of which now we know almost nothing), so presumably *Regulus* was one of the very few stars visible in the days when we had two suns in our sky.

We noted in Chapter 6 (see: *Aldebaran*) that *Regulus* is one of the four Archangel stars, Raphael, the Healing Archangel. The last Leonine era in our history, in the immediate aftermath of a cosmic disaster, was undoubtedly a period when the whole structure of life on Earth was critically in need of healing in the medical as well as any more profound esoteric and spiritual sense.

In other cultures also, those same four stars in the 'Fixed Signs' of the Zodiac were regarded as especially exalted: The Four Royal Stars or The Four Guardians of Heaven in the more religious cultures. They have also been characterised as Horses from time to time, and we see their respective astrological attributes reflected both in the famed Four Horsemen of the Apocalypse (Revelations, 6) and the Chariot Horses in the Book of Zechariah.

In that latter telling, (Zech, 6), there is a piece of astronomical information which few of us today would believe to have been known so long ago: the Bay horses went back and forth from East to West, their colour matching Aldebaran and Antares, the guardians of those quarters respectively. The Grisled horse went South, a fair colour-match for Fomalhaut. The White went North, and what other way to describe Regulus, 50,000 times brighter than the Sun. And the *Black Horse* went North too, ahead of the White. Regulus has a little known companion star, some 3' of arc from it, described as 'as if steeped in indigo', and 'discovered' by astronomers only close to our own times! It seems this forebear of 'dark horses' is not such a recent discovery after all. The dark one, by the bye, was found by Winlock to be itself a double with only 3 secs of arc between them.
Regulus was long considered the supreme of the Four Guardians, but the role of *Fomalhaut* – Gabriel, in the birth of Jesus – must now be said to challenge or actually supplant, with a new stage in human spiritual evolution, the supremacy of the more 'medical' Archangel of the Leonine era.

The Sign of **(Leo)**, however, remains the great symbol of healing for astrologers looking for a hopeful prospect on the chart of an ailing client, and its ruler, the Sun, is the prime planet of health. It is no accident that **Leo's** chief star,

Regulus, is not only the symbol of Raphael but also 'The Star of Kings'. Right up to the beginnings of modern western democracy, say 1776 to 1789 AD., it was taken for granted that kings had power to heal, and one disease especially was called 'the king's evil', because only the touch of the monarch was considered able to cure one of it. In principle, this still holds in the present day – if one can get past the bureaucracy on the way!

In Chapter Three, we discussed the royal connotations of *Regulus* at length and it suffices now just to repeat in summary that rulers with or without crowns only stay safely in office while they make it their business to care for and enrich their subjects, at least in fair proportion to their own good fortunes. And this is becoming an ever stronger obligation upon them, even the most absolute monarchs, as *Regulus* nears its transition in Sign from **(Leo)** to **(Virgo)**, where we shall find it from the year 2018 AD. **(Virgo's)** quality of obligation to be of service to others, under their watchful and critical assessment of the service given, will then exercise full force where *Regulus* is concerned, and it may be something less than the almost automatically 'good star' that we have held it to be hitherto. But, where the obligations that go with it are met, it will still be the star that promises long life, good fortune, high office and esteem.

Denebola, β Leonis, is next on our list, the second brightest in the Constellation and easy to see in the sky without optical aids. The name comes from *Al Danab Al Asad*. The Tail of the Lion, so Danabala. It lies 22° past *Regulus* (the Lion faces backwards in the Zodiac) and so it has been in **(Virgo)** since about 300 AD.

Ptolemy gave *Denebola* a Saturn-Venus quality, which must make it at least mildly 'Benefic' even in traditional astrology, since Venus was held to be the only planet that could really get along with Saturn. The tails of the celestial creatures are at least as important as their heads, being in some cases their weaponry (Scorpio), in others their means of communication (Cetus, the Whale), in others their link to the past and of course, sometimes 'the part we don't talk about'!

The Lion's tail has the quality of being farthest from the end that one should not approach unwarily, and so it has a venusian quality of peace and safety about it, but we should still not be tempted into 'pulling the lion's tail', as vernacular saying has wisely warned. Therein lies the Saturn quality of *Denebola*.

We should expect, therefore, that this star symbolises strength from the Lion, along with both the ability and the need to use it wisely and constructively. There should also be the note of looking forward while at the same time being able to draw upon past experience, gained at the head end of the animal, so to say, since this Lion faces back down the Zodiac, as already remarked. Perhaps the 'achilles heel' of monarchs, even the most progressive of them, is that their positions are so much steeped in past tradition that it is all too difficult to come forward from it, even if they want to. Thus, from this special forward-looking attribute of *Denebola*, we might well ponder that one with this star strong in the horoscope is at least as well favoured, and possibly more so, in our times – than with the mighty *Regulus* at his service. And those are indeed the qualities of *Denebola*.

In other cultures, it has had a few different titles; even one Arab, Kaswini, called it The Lion's Bowels (Al Akrab Al Asad) instead of the tail, since the latter lies swept a little alongside its owner and the tip is thus in the bowel region. To another Arab, Ụlug Beg, it was Al Sarfah, The Changer, meaning that the weather turned cold when the star rose, warmer as it vanished from the night sky again. A latinisation of that name was Mutatrix. To the Hindus, it was the main star of the asterism Uttara Phalguni, and Al Biruni records Hindus telling him that the horoscope of their celebrated scientist Vahara Mihira had the Moon on this asterism, well befitting *Denebola's* reputation for future orientated thinking. Others have called it 'Blue Star', its actual colour, and 'The Burning One', probably a similar reference to the extreme heat of blue stars. By any name or standard *Denebola* is a fine lively member of the celestial family.

We now come to several lesser stars, but still worthy of note, in the Lion's head, neck and mane. *Algeiba* is γ Leonis, nominally third brightest in **Leo**, though today's astronomers rate it slightly brighter than *Denebola*, with a magnitude of 1.99. In fact it is a widely spaced Binary, almost more an Optical Double, of two stars with Mags, 2.3 and 3.5 respectively, whence the combined brightness greater than either one of them. Much confusion reigns about the name, and how to pronounce it, for it is close both in name and position to *Al Jabbah* (The Mane) and it may be that only later commentators troubled to separate the two stars. In that case the G and J in both names are pronounced as our S in 'measure'. But others say that the Arabs got the word from the Latin 'Juba' (Mane), in which case pronounce as in 'Jugoslavia'. G as in 'Gun' is out. Although Ptolemy seems to have given it a Saturn-Mercury quality, if again that wasn't *Al Jabbah*, it is hard to know why he bothered, for it lies only 21 minutes of arc short of *Regulus* in longitude. We may say, therefore, that it contributes both authority and wisdom to The Star of Kings, as indeed kings surely need, and we may continue to say it phonetically: *Al Jayba*, to distinguish it from *Al Jabbah*.

We pass over δ Leonis for a moment to say a few words on *Al Jabbah*, η Leonis. Also in the Lion's Mane (see above), it is another Saturn-Mercury star, not quite 2° short of *Regulus*, and so again adding its qualities to that star, as does *Algeiba*. Perhaps this IS the moment to say a negative word about Saturn-Mercury stars, especially if not favourably aspected on a chart: like the two planets themselves when harshly aspected, there can be a tendency either to talk one's way into troubles, or to be less than truthful, or harsh in judgement on others. Not all 'hard' aspects should be taken so negatively without further consideration, however. The Square in particular may show up some of those features, or it may show more positively a capacity for painstaking thought and slow deliberation before making a decision. A still harder aspect (e.g: Sesquisquare) may show that deliberation to be generally too slow for the needs of the occasion, or even downright procrastination.

The remaining star in the Lion's neck or mane is *Adhafera*, ζ Leonis, the name derived, so far as the author can cope with an Arabic dictionary, from *Al Thafara* (TH as in That, not in Thick) meaning that this is at the back of the Lion's ear. So *Athafera* is a fairly right pronunciation. Being so close to the others within the orb of *Regulus*, it is no surprise that Ptolemy again makes this a Saturn-Mercury star. But the position and name imply listening carefully, rather than having too much to say, and this is surely a useful quality with which to precede the more voluble or loquacious attributes of *Al Jabbah*, *Al Geiba* and *Regulus* itself. Someone with *Adhafera*'s degree strong on their horoscope, then, either is a good listener, if well aspected, or needs to practise becoming one if the aspect is difficult.

Now we move up fully into the Lion's head, where we find a pair of stars, shown in some astronomical books by the mixed Arabic-Latin names: *Ar Ras Al Asad Borealis*, and *Ar Ras al Asad Australis*; or The Head of the Lion (North), and ditto (South). To make all that a little less ugly linguistically, we should either put them fully into Latin: *Caput Leonis Borealis* and *Australis*, or in Arabic: *Ar Ras Al Asad As Shamali* (North), and *Ar Ras Al Asad Al Janubi* (South).

The Northern one, μ Leonis, is in fact little used in astrology but it does sometimes appear under the name *Al Ashfar*, the Eyebrows, or sometimes as *Al Schemali*, a poor attempt at saying North, and easily confused with the much better known star of similar barbarised name in Scorpio (q.v). So, if the reader wants to use it, *Al Ashfar* is the best title and the quality of looking carefully at a situation before forging ahead into it is what we should read here. Ptolemy has not helped us on this one, but Saturn-Mars would be the general idea.

The Southern head star, ε Leonis, is much more familiar, as *El Genubi (Al Janubi)*, but again this leads to confusion with the same in Scorpio, which is why the latter is more often called South Scale (and the northern one there is likewise called North Scale). It too has been sometimes called Al Ashfar, since it is also in the eyebrow region of the Lion, but probably we do best to keep to the name given at the start of this paragraph, no matter that it is a bit lacking in obvious meaning. *El Genubi* is listed by Ptolemy as a Saturn-Mars type, again giving the qualitative connotations we saw with its neighbour *Al Ashfar.*

We have one more major star in **Leo** to deal with, variously called *Dhur* or *Zosma* in most books and lists. *Dhur* derives from Al Thahr, The Back, or Al Thuhur, The Backs, since this star, δ Leonis, is sometimes given plurally with Θ Leonis: the pair of them are situated almost one above the other on the Lion's hindquarters.

The alternative name *Zosma* is a Greek rendering of an old Persian name meaning Girdle. Still other names have included Al Kahil Al Asad, the part of the back between the shoulder blades, and (for the two stars together) Al H'aratan – the two small ribs. Even Al Zubrah, another word for the mane, has been applied to both stars at some times. We must assume from all this that the Lion has not always been seen the way we see it now. Possibly it was depicted sitting upright, and enlarged to include at least some of what is now **Leo Minor**, above the present constellation. It matters not over much: *Dhur* (Thur, with Th as in Then) or *Zosma*, if that is easier to say, are the common titles now.

It is well visible to the naked eye, Mag.2.58, and is in fact a tight group of three stars to make it optically a 'triple'. It has Ptolemy's fairly unusual classification as a Saturn-Venus type, like *Denebola* not too far from it, and must therefore be considered as of somewhat the same nature. It holds a position of quite some strength in the Lion's anatomy (along with Θ, of course) and can thus be seen as a source of strength in a horoscope – a source to be used in the very practical manner of its placing in **(Virgo)**, where it has been since about 1050 AD, showing a somewhat critical turn of mind but with a constructive intent behind it so long as the aspect and the planet on it in the horoscope are in harmony with it.

If that be not the case then *Dhur-Zosma* is calling for the cultivation of constructiveness if the subject of the horoscope wants to live life harmoniously. Given that proviso, it is generally held to be 'benefic' by any authority, most of whom go so far as to promise high government or managerial office on account of it. Mars seems to be the one planet not too welcome in conjunction with *Dhur*, the critical 'I know better than everyone else' attitude being hardest to overcome then. But if it is overcome, then this star as a source of strength in situations demanding hard work can well be at its very best. Like all else in the heavens, it only shows what we have in us to use wisely and beneficially; it does not force us in how we actually use those tools.

And that completes our survey of **Leo**, the big bright Constellation of the northern summertime, though of course it is then hidden in daylight, a cheering reminder to us in winter that we are not abandoned and that summer will come again. Somehow both the big lion and Raphael the Archangel of Healing seem comforting presences at the time of year when our spate of colds and 'flu finds us most in need of strength and help from the 'Great Doctor Up There'.

CHAPTER 10

Virgo the Maiden

The sixth Sign of the Zodiac, **(Virgo)** is also the second of the 'Human' Signs and, like the first of these, **(Gemini)**, it is ruled by Mercury, the planet associated with human intelligence and communication. But where **(Gemini)** is generally thought of as the child, acquiring basic knowledge and first learning to communicate intelligibly, **(Virgo)** has more the connotation of the grown human who has stored what has been learned and now puts it to work at the service of fellow humanity. So it has come about that this is the Sign of Service, Work-Employment, and the kindred matters of Food and Physical Health. It is accounted a feminine Sign, as are all the even-numbered Signs (even the Bull!), but not especially on account of its name.

As a Constellation, **Virgo** is not one of the more impressive sights to the unaided eye, having only one star, *Spica*, which is outstanding. We shall be listing five others here, four of which are reasonably visible without optical aids. A good way to locate **Virgo** in the Spring night sky is to begin with the handle of the *Plough*, follow its curve steadily downwards to the large bright star *Arcturus* (in *Böotes*) and then continue, slightly flattening the curve to arrive at *Spica*, almost as large, and actually brighter, some two thirds of the way through the constellation towards the western, Libran, end.

As with nearly all the most ancient contellations, **Virgo** has enough fine stories attached to her to fill a book all by herself. We must be sparing here and, hopefully, tell enough to give us a clear feel of the Zodiac's 'First Lady', without losing ourselves in too many tales.

Probably the most popular story comes to us via the Greek writer Hesiod, for whom **Virgo** was Astraea ('she of the stars'), goddess of Justice, daughter of Jupiter and Themis, in the 'Golden Era' when the gods in person walked the Earth and ruled here. She was the last of the gods to leave us, and only went when she saw how repulsively we had changed our behaviour quite suddenly. (The only judge ever to have resigned in protest over crime!).

That myth contains several interesting features for us: The 'Golden Era' (or 'Age') takes us back before the loss of *Phaethon*, of course, and so we find again the implication that natives of other planets, with probably superior intellects to the earthlings of the time, came here and had power to rule. There is also, again, the note of some profound mutation happening to our ancestors after the stellar explosion so that, with the more general destruction upon this planet as well, we became at least a poor investment, or even quite ungovernable. And then, too, there is the implication that some part of this Constellation – most probably the prime star *Spica*, close to the Ecliptic – was visible from Earth during the brief twilight between the two suns. Yet further note of interest is that this goddess, as 'minister of justice', would seem to be more associated with **Libra** than with **Virgo**.

Here we arrive at the widely (though not universally) held contention that **Libra** is a comparatively recent (Roman) addition to the constellations, and that what are now **Virgo**, **Libra** & **Scorpio** was once a single continuous configuration. There is much to support this view. The very idea of symbolising justice by a set of weighing scales stems from the early concern of law with fair trading in corn, the prime significance in many cultures of this constellation of the harvest season, and the harvest goddess, Demeter (Ceres), sister of Astraea, has also been equated with **Virgo**.

But, in ancient China, this same constellation was both the Serpent and the Phoenix, symbols of procreation and of death-and-self-resurrection, which themes we associate especially with **Scorpio**. The close similarity of the glyphs for the two constellations, as Zodiac Signs, is clear enough: MP and MU as best they can be put into our letters, and it may be a surprise to see that the glyph for **Libra** fits between them to make a very meaningful glyph for one large constellation: MP Ω MU. If this be drawn by hand, it easily becomes a long undulating snake, its tail in the U, its middle humped over a tree branch, Ω, around the trunk, P, and finishing in the adjoining M. What have we then but the tempting serpent, Satan, in the 'tree of life', a truly Scorpionic theme, which is also the tree of 'Knowledge of good and evil', the Libran judicical keynote, tempting Eve who is yet another lady often associated with **Virgo**.

And all that finds further support in Sumerian-Chaldean astrology, in which **Virgo**, and especially its prime star *Spica*, was the supreme goddess of Creation (or *Pro*creation), Ishtar, or Istar. Apart from being the name from which come the words Aster and Star, high tribute indeed to the goddess's exalted station, Ishtar is also the origin of the Hebrew Ashtoreth, from which then the Greek Aphrodite, also the goddess of procreation.

The theme is developed further yet in the Assyrian culture where **Virgo** was Baalita, wife of the god Baal, of notoriety in Hebrew lore; then again we find her in Babylonian myth to be Mylitta (Molutta), Queen of the Night, worship of whom was roundly condemned by the Hebrew prophet Jeremiah (Jer.XLIV, 17-19). This dark queen is often now confused with the Moon, Luna, but was in fact Lilith, the satellite which Earth had before Luna, and the female demon,

Adam's unfaithful wife of Hebrew lore.

This traditional 'wicked witch' figure is familiar to us in the 'Snow White' story, holding up a mirror to her own perfection, only to be told by it that there is another (Eve) still fairer than her, and the P of the MP glygh for **Virgo** is sometimes said to represent that mirror. Another contention, however, is that the glyph is really the Greek Παρ (Par to us), the initial syllable of Παρθєνos (Parthenos), another of **Virgo's** titles and suggesting that Lilith represents a dim record in us of a time before the Great Catastrophe, when our ancestors were androgynous or hermaphrodite, rather than hetero-aphrodite as we are now, and parthenogenetic in the production of offspring. It is noteworthy that the birth stories of our great avatar or saviour figures, Jesus now the most honoured of them, feature parthenogenesis as their origin. Not surprisingly, the Virgin Mary has become another holder of title to **Virgo**, since about the 12th Century A.D.

In early Arab astrology the eastern stars of **Virgo** were included in a **Leo** *(Al Asad)* somewhat larger than ours, but, by Islamic times, their savants had conformed to the European configuration and *Virgo* was then called Al Athra Al Nathifah, The Chaste Maiden. It has also been called Al Sunbulah, the Wheatsheaf, however, since it is not done to make portrayals of human form in any way that might induce temptation to worship a false god, so that **Virgo** was illustrated by them as the sheaf of corn so often found in the lady's hands in western drawings. And now that we and safely say we have the 'feel' of **Virgo**, we can go on to look at her chief stars.

Spica, α Virginis, must surely be first on our list, even though it lies far towards the end of the constellation, and is currently at 23° of **(Libra)**, which Sign it entered in about 5 BC. Some readers may like to ponder the significance of The Virgin's change of Sign just at the birth of her Son, widely thought to have been in 4 BC. *Spica*, as already said, is one of the truly great stars in the sky, the one which gave us our word 'star', and at least as important as the four archangel stars. It is very bright, magnitude 0.9, and very hot, spectral class B2, and inspection with a telescope reveals it to be a Binary with the two components only about three million miles apart, and orbiting each other in about four days of our time. It is not a fully 'eclipsing' Binary – the one component does not fully obscure the other as we see them – but the magnitude does vary between about 0.9 and 1.0. It is one of several major stars actually approaching us, at some 9.2 miles per second, not a matter for urgent action on our part yet: it is still about 260 light-years away, so we have 5 million years in hand before life gets to be too bright for comfort here!!

Spica is on the Virgin's left hand and is almost universally seen as the ear of wheat she holds, which is what the name means. Only among the pre-Islamic Arabs was it held to be in the shin or calf of their very large lion constellation; now they call it Sunbalah, with the same meaning as our name for it. The astronomer Al Biruni called it Al Hulbah, The Bristle, probably because the wheat usually portrayed is of that spiky kind, like barley, as the word Spica suggests also. The considerable distance between *Spica* and its nearest neighbours has inspired some cultures to call it 'The Lonely One' and names like that, often to distinguish it from the equally prominent *Arcturus*, on almost the same Zodiacal longitude but higher in the sky and much closer to its neighbours in *Bootes* (q.v.).

Astrologically, *Spica* is a 'Good Star', and no doubt it still is, if we don't contemplate our descendants' fates in 5 million years' time. Our friend classified it as a Venus-Mars type, the only one of that kind. This combination of the opposite sexes in the one star must inspire a further thought about the androgynous qualities we have already noted with **Virgo**, but it is doubtful that Ptolemy noted that. As the star of the grain harvest, it is the provider of our material needs, and indeed it always does show up well in that respect. There is, however, a word of warning to go with it: We only reap harvest if we have first sown the seed and cared for the fields, and what we reap must last us, and all who laboured in our fields, until the next harvest is ready. He does not do so well from *Spica* who reaps what he has not sown, uses it profligately, or denies to others their share in his good fortune. As though to rub this in quite firmly, *Arcturus* in the sky above the Virgin's Hand is the prime star of the much rougher character, the Herdsman, just as ready to take care of his herd but not to stand any nonsense from them.

Spica is also noted for its spirtual and religious qualities, as we must expect after all we have seen about **Virgo**, and indeed people with this star strong in their horoscopes do very often gain high place in those fields of life. (Even the famous Biblical mystery word 'Shibboleth' gets a look in: it is the old Hebrew name for *Spica*, and likewise means an ear of wheat.) Psychic awareness is also above average in such people, especially if the more sensitive planets, Moon, Venus, Neptune or Lilith are conjunct with *Spica*.

The second star of **Virgo** by Greek-letter rating, β Virginis, is not actually the second brightest; it's current visual magnitude is 3.8, whereas there are serveral others between 2.9 and 3. This star is alternatively named *Zavijava* or *Al Araf* (or *Araph*). Currently at 26° 56' of the Sign, which is at only 0°50' into the Constellation, it is not surprising that Ptolemy gave it the very Leonine qualities of a Mercury-Mars star. Of the names, *Zavijava* probably derives from Al Zawiyah which among other things means a small Mosque subsidiary to a larger one nearby. Since such a Mosque is very much a symbol of authority in its locality, as a parish church is in other communities, the idea conveyed here is of someone holding a position of command but subject to a higher command behind them.

Al Araf conveys the same notion in another way, being a much diminshed corruption of an original which meant: 'Those who send forth (others to carry out their orders)', or: 'Those who are SENT forth. . . .'. That seems a very logical notion for the star which carries us on from **Leo**, symbol of commanding others, into **Virgo** where we work for those who have command over us. The Mercury-Mars quality perhaps suggests more of the **Leo** nature, the intelligent director behind the action, but the name can just as well imply that 'the successful applicant will work in the field on his own initiative, directly responsible to the M.D.', as current top-job adverts put the matter. The planetary simile therefore suggests one who has the intelligence and energy to be sent out and not need the king there to lead him all the time.

And so the qualities we find in people with this star very precisely engaged upon their horoscopes (it is faint, with small orb), are those of a reliable worker, attentive to every detail of the job, able to control this if the star and its companion planet is well aspected, so that he will make a good salesman, executive, manager or subordinate commander, but needs someone of higher rank to have given him the job. If less well aspected he can be that sort of underling who provokes his men to strike or mutiny by over-playing the 'little Hitler' act. His own downfall is then assured. If he does have that harder aspect there, however, he can best use it by avoiding control over others, taking on instead something like painstaking research in difficult fields where there are few people or sources to guide him.

Several more stars, not in the Zodiadcal constellations, lie very close to *Al Araf* by longitude: *Labrum*, the lip of *Crater* the cup; *Al Kaid*, the *Head Man* in the locality, an *Ursa Major* star; and *Markeb* the Boat, in the **Argo** constellation. All these have to do with swearing loyalty to another, taking charge under him, and 'running the ship' for him.

The next star we come to by longitude is *Zaniah*, η Virginis, now at 4°34' in **(Libra)**, 10°7' **Virgo**. Despite its Greek rating it is, at Vis.Mag. 2.95, a little brighter than *Al Araf*. Ptolemy rates this one as a Mercury-Venus type, quite a compliment to it since Mercury is ruler of the Constellation while Venus rules the Sign. The name must bring a smile to astrologers who (often quite rightly) associate Mercury with money and Venus with love, and with Ptolemy having put the money first, for Zaniyah means Adulteress or Harlot. We have already seen how **Virgo** has had such a reputation in past times, having been Lilith and Ashtoreth as much as more honoured ladies like Mary. A little amusement is also permissible on reading older books in which either the word is not translated at all, or the authors digress into a learned discussion on whether or not this star belongs to a group once known as the Kennels, along with the 'little mosque'. Victorian avoidance of the unmentionable does have its comic side!

The more positive attributes of *Zaniah*, however, can be seen in the Mercury-Venus-in-Libra talent for negotiating peace. One attribute which a good commander (or salesman), *Al Araf*, must surely need is an intuition for knowing when to call a halt to battle and either offer or seek terms for peace. And if well aspected and on the right planet, Mercury, Venus, Sun or Jupiter, for example, this is just what will show up on an horoscope. With Saturn or Mars the terms for peace may be too harsh for acceptance; with Moon or Neptune they may be either unrealistic or downright 'shady', especially with harsh aspects there. So, as usual, how 'good' or 'bad' *Zaniah* is, depends very clearly on how we are.

A little way on again, we come to one of the much better-known stars in astrology, indeed one of the truly renowned: 'She of the Grape Harvest', *Vindemiatrix*, ϵ Virginis. Its present position is at 9°40' **(Libra)**, or 15°7' **Virgo**, thus at the very centre of the Constellation. It is not often called now by its Arabic name, *Al Muredin*, but we shall not leave that unmentioned here.

In older astrology this star ranks with *Algol* in having an unmitigated reputation for evil, and some have even noted that the arc or aspect between the two is the much feared 135°, the sesqui-quadrate or sesquisquare. But the underlying reason for their similar reputes lies in the connection of both names with the theme of 'the Spirit'. The one is the name from which comes our word Alcohol, the other is the star whose rising signifies the time for harvesting the grapes, our main old source of the same.

As always, much depends on how one sees events themselves as good or bad. Yes, it does frequently mark the death of someone's partner in life, whence its appellation 'The

Widow Maker', which of course prompts us to say: 'It is bound to, since someone dies at every minute or so of every day'. But still the fact remains that it figures very strongly and very regularly in deaths which are in some way dramatic, newsworthy or are resented in much more than the usual degree by those left behind (assassinations, common criminal murders, executions, airline disasters etc.). At least one unsafe airplane of World War II, known widely as 'The Widow Maker' made its first flight on the day that *Vindemiatrix* culminated, while another which had the same phenomenon at its birth, but was successful, was officially named the 'Black Widow'!

On this topic, an author must always remember that someone may be reading his book just as they have suffered a loss, and he should not be trite on what is not personally affecting him at this moment. But it is a fact that all major creeds teach that death is a rich harvesting of the Spirit, with life of some rewarding kind beyond it, and that such a teaching is indeed the truth. The 'bad star' label pinned on *Vindemiatrix* does, then, have to be seen in this light, hard though it is to see it thus when the emotional stress is greatest. If the emotions are allowed their necessary free expression at first, but followed by recognition of this truth, then the sad event can become a spiritual enrichment for the bereaved as much as for the one gone on.

This is the right moment to mention again the alternative name of this star: *Al Muredin*, very like 'The One Sent Forth', *Al Araf*, but here with the added connotation of being sent forth in 'The Faith', the *Ed Diin* portion of the name. This is very much more the missionary or the apostle than the soldier or salesman, and this is strongly hinted in the Ptolemaic Saturn-Mercury simile for this star, by contrast with the Mercury-Mars of *Al Araf*.

That is not to say that everyone with this star strong on the horoscope must go out and preach the gospel to the heathen, although many do indeed feel a strong religious calling, but as a practising counsellor the author always does advise such people to look carefully at the motives and integrity of what they do, whether it be preaching, soldiering or selling. Are they satisfied that they are serving their fellow man, with sound counselling, genuine defence of the peace, a sound and satisfactory product that the buyer really does need, or are they exploiting his credulity and wealth for their own ends? *Al Muredin/Vindemiatrix* is a sign of success in the one case, disaster in the other. What they sow they will surely harvest.

Only one fifth of a degree from *Vindemiatrix* is the star *Porrima*, or *Antevorta*, or *Postvorta*, or *Prorsa*, or *Zawiat Al Awwa*, or *Kafir (Caphir)*, γ Virginis. It is not open to further bids to christen it!

This must seem extraordinary to the astrologer, for whom the star is virtually indistinguishable from its predecessor, but there is a big difference in their declinations, *Vindemiatrix* being the lady's upraised hand while *Porrima* is under her reclining back. Between the two, in fact is a third star, δ Virginis, *Minelauva/Minalawwa*, on her tummy, which is not noted for use in astrology.

The titles *Porrima* through *Prorsa* all refer to two early goddesses of prediction, much favoured by the Romans, which must alone account for them taking any note of this star at all. And the Arabic title *Kafir* (Infidel) for it no doubt springs from Islamic revulsion against pagan goddesses. The other Arabic title *Zawiat Al Awwa* means 'Temple, or Mosque, at the Corner', for the star does indeed lie on a marked bend in the figure of the constellation as a whole. The third star's name, *Minalawwa*, simply means 'From (away from) the Corner'. If we wish to give significance to δ Virginis as *Porrima* etc., then the theme must be that it emphasises the common obession of predictors with the death connotations of *Vindemiatrix*, while, as *Kafir*, it is a reminder to the missionary in *Al Muredin* that he is going out to meet the pagan devotees of sundry gods and goddesses. Its Mercury-Venus classification by Ptolemy, coupled with the Saturn-Mercury of *Muredin*, is remarkably akin to the Quran with its regular alternation of promises of peace and reward to the faithful, and stern warnings to those who continue in their paganism. So it is itself both warning to the would-be missonary of what he must confront, advice on the peace he should preach, and promise of the reward that awaits his labours.

One more major star concerns us now: *Khambaliȧ*, λ Virginis. It is a Mercury-Mars star by Ptolemy. The name has its roots in old Coptic and means 'Crooked Claw', most probably the same device which we call also the Swastika, and whose ancient symbolism contained the idea of a secret knowledge, accessible to us, but only if one knows the way to get to it, as we find also with the symbolism of the maze in other cultures. The word 'Shambala' has a similar root and meaning; so has the pentagram, so that the Arabic word for Five, Khamsa, may well also derive from the same piece of mystique. Khamr, wine, also has a connection, being so often a symbol for the 'secret of life', 'the Spirit' again, as well as the means so often used to enter a transcendental (or just inebriated) state of consciousness. Both Sufi and Alchemical literature are of course rich in this allegorical form.

So *Khambalia* is very much a star of the penetration of secrets and, although within the Constellation of Virgo by the map, its present location by Sign is at 6°38' of **(Scorpio)**, 'a long way from home', and at 12°11' **Libra** even when we have corrected its sidereal placing. So the Mars in the simile which Ptolemy gave it is that of Mars in its second rulership, rather than the open energy of Aries. Consequently this star denotes those good at applying intellect to deep research of any kind, to police-type investigation, to espionage, and also to such pursuits as alchemy and the esoteric in general.

If two horoscopes each have a strong feature, the one on this star, the other opposite to it, there is evidence to suggest that the relationship between the two can appear quite malefic on the surface, yet with a deep understanding of each other, even a willing co-operation at a deep subliminal level, it is as though their apparent conflict is part of an act by which both are together finding the way to the source of their Being, the centre of that swastika in them. It is hoped that readers have by now ceased to associate the swastika with the regime that briefly made it notorious from 1933 to 1945.

Khambalia has a very close neighbour by longitude, just as we saw with Vindemiatrix and Kafir, but in this case the companion star is less well known and does not appear to have been included by Ptolemy. The extra star here is i Virginis, *Syrma*, or *Surma*, by its Greek titles, *Al Ghafar* by its more meaningful name in Arabic. The significance of this star and title lies firstly in the heavy personal responsibility which is implicit in the occult questing and acquisition of spiritual power seen in *Khambalia*, and secondly in the Islamic concept of *Istighafar*.

Ghafar means to cover and to protect, and to suppress. The longer word is a recognition that the greater our attainment of spiritual power, or indeed any power at all, since all is given to us by God, then the more serious are our lapses into error and sin, to which we remain prone, no matter what power, even the most spiritual, we attain. Some would rephrase that to say *especially* the most spiritual. So it becomes more than ever necessary that we should keep up a close dialogue with God through prayer, and actively request His correction of our course at every moment, before errors build up into a major deviation from which recovery becomes too difficult. It is rather like the pilot of a light plane not having to worry too soon about a compass error, while he who flies a supersonic type can go far astray in a matter of minutes.

This star *Ghafar,* then, is a vitally needed companion to *Khambalia* which, all in all, is a star of the very deepest significance and a challenge which those blessed or afflicted with it on their horoscopes just cannot resist taking up.

Now we leave **Virgo,** Lady of the Zodiac, Sign of applied human intellect, and in ancient pagan lore the Queen of the Heavens entire. For all its general faintness in the sky, *Spica* excepted, it is amazingly rich in galaxies for the astronomer, and meaning for the astrologer who would truly seek the Divine in his/her art.

CHAPTER 11

Libra the Balance

Libra, Sign or Constellation, is noteworthy as the 'mechanical sign', a manufactured device, and thus in some opinions not a truly qualified member of the *Zoo - diac,* not a living animal or human.

We saw in the last chapter how the three Signs **(Virgo, Libra, Scorpio)** seem once to have been a single figure until this was broken up when **Libra** was carved from its middle. Some accounts blame or credit Julius Caesar for this, though there is considerable evidence that it was done some long time before him. It does not matter a great deal; **Libra** is a fairly recent introduction into the Zodiac, its main stars taken from what was earlier **Scorpio,** and they still bear names connected to that Sign and Constellation, alongside of the names given to them since.

Its recent origin does not diminish its astrological authenticity or importance in any way, however. As the seventh Sign, and the opposite of the first, it characterises that point of life when we are made to see ourselves by contrasting the subjective image we have been nursing with the reality of the surrounding world and how others put their view of us before our faces. It is thus regarded as the first of the 'objective' Signs, those from **(Libra)** through **(Pisces)**, fair enough so long as one remembers that astrology as a whole is very much a subjective art per se.

Only two of the stars here are commonly given much attention: *South Scale,* α Librae, and *North Scale,* β Librae. As their names imply, they mark the scale-pans of the weighing-balance that **Libra** is. But each is just as well known by another name: *South Scale* is *Zuban Al Janubi* (or *El Genubi)*; *North Scale* is *Zuban Al Shamali* (*El Schemali*), these meaning respectively the South and North Claw (of *the Scorpion.*)

Frequently the 'Zuban' gets dropped, leaving rather without meaning just the Arabic words for South and North, and causing some confusion with ϵ Leonis, the southern star in **Leo's** head, which gets shortened likewise to just *El Genubi.* Some authors, astronomical as well as astrological, have inexcusably mistaken south for north and confused millions of readers!

Before we look at the significance of these two stars in horoscopy, it will help if we give the other major names by which they are sometimes called in older literature: *South Scale*, actually a pair of stars in wide Binary combination, is occasionally called *Al Kiffa Al Janubi,* meaning simply South Tray, or Scale, in Arabic. It is also called *Al Mizan Alalyamin*, Mizan being the verb to fill up a skin as in a crude balance with goatskin at each end of the beam to receive the goods and checkweights. Alalyamin means 'on the Right'. *Al Wazn Al Janubi* is yet another title: The Southern Weight. Yet another is the Babylonian title *Nuru Sha Shutu*, The Southern Light, and again this may be found in early Arabic as *Al Nur Al Janubi*. We sometimes come across ugly hybrid forms of these names, where the Arabic first word has been suffixed by *Australis*, the Latin for South.

North Scale has received similar treatment, with *Al Shamali* in place of *Al Janubi*, of course, and the same word or *Yasar* also means Left. The Babylonian is *Nuru Sha Iltanu,* while *Borealis*, Latin for North sometimes appears too.

South Scale, situated now at 14°32' (**Scorpio**), 20°21' **Libra**, was classed by Ptolemy as a Jupiter-Mars star, not unfitting for the prime star in the Sign which has so much to do with justice, whose feminine personification on the dome of London's 'Old Bailey' court is a lady with the scales of Libra in one hand, the martian sword in the other. Jupiter is much associated with the authority of the Supreme Judge, fair and merciful, even though he must point the sword to the guilty, beneficent to the plaintiff who has been wronged.

Not that human judges always measure up to that high ideal, and that means all of us in our judgement of others, not just those paid for the job. *South Scale* as an astrological feature contains all of that allegory: well aspected and on the 'right' planet in a horoscope, we have someone of courage to fight for the right, but generosity to his opponents when they are defeated. If harshly aspected, especially to Mars, Saturn or Moon, justice may well take a back seat behind vengeance. Such a person does well not to get into any kind of job where he can use this power, for surely he will himself live to regret it in public dishonour or worse.

It is well to remember here the other association of this star with a scorpion's claw, used for making love as well as for slaying its prey. It does not let go until the one or the other matter is complete, and onlookers are often not sure which of the two acts is actually in process. Sometimes even the scorpion seems to get it wrong along the way! Humans engaged in relationship with others, marital, judicious or whatever, need to keep very clear heads and hearts if this star is strong with them. It frequently shows up ill-aspected in many unfortunate situations, from domestic strife and miscarriages of justice, to psychopathic killings that started out in the guise of love. But again, its appearance in better aspect is often just the right moment to repair a relationship and to reconsider an earlier harsh judgement.

North Scale, currently at 19°10' (**Scorpio**), 24°42' **Libra**, is a Jupiter-Mercury star in Ptolemy's book. Although this must sound quite innocuous compared with the Jupiter-Mars of the other Scale, this star does in fact rank very high among the 'malefics' of traditional astrology. The reasoning behind this lies, however, in the degree on which it stands, rather than with the star. It is known ominously as 'The Accursed Degree of the Accursed Sign', for it is recorded in ancient history as the degree on which the Earth was struck by the storm of debris from the explosion of Phaethon, and life was all but extinguished on this planet. Since this event, not generally believed by modern 'scientists' to have really happened, it forms a large part of that 'secret knowledge' to which we referred in connection with *Khambalia* in our Virgo chapter, and a very large part too in the most deeply buried psychological and physical ills rampant among us all. It quite certainly is a difficult spot for us, all superstition apart.

The star itself is much noted for particular sharpness of mind and intellect and, according to what planets, house and aspects are found with it on the horoscope, there is often a very powerful psychic quality there also – or psychotic if the planets and aspects are of a harsh enough nature. This is just what we must expect from the simile of a Jupiter-Mercury conjunction: for good or ill it will go to the extremes of what a human mind can achieve. Again, as with *South Scale*, the companion theme of the Scorpion's Claw leaves an open question as to what the creature is doing, loving or killing, and whether it is clear about the difference in its own mind!

The Sun was on *North Scale* on the day World War I ended, but on 'The Accursed Degree' exactly the next day, when the way was open for the onerous terms of the 'peace treaty', resentment of whose blatant injustice was such a spur to the rebirth of German militarism, and thus to World War II. In the previous year, 1917, Sun was on *South Scale* for the 'October Revolution' (Nov. 7th) in Russia. Of course it was on *North Scale*, and then on 19 (**Scorpio**) before the situation had settled, but still one wonders if a less harsh and uncomprising stance by the victorious Bolsheviki would not have favoured them well in the days and years which were to follow.

As a last comment on *North Scale* and its notorious degree, the lady Kim, to whom this book is dedicated, had a Sun-Neptune conjunction right on it, in her 12th house, prelude to a short and very troubled life of only 22 years, but with the most remarkable psychic powers and the privilege of knowing the precise date, to the minute, of her death nine years before it happened.

Poppy, who shares the dedication, hardly left Kim's side for the last three years, and died with her in a road accident at the same age after an almost equally troubled life. She shared the Neptune position, and had her Part of Marriage (Companionship) exactly opposite to it. She also manifested much of the same psychic ability from the time that the two came together as nurses and comforters of the dying during the final hours, using their psychic gifts, sometimes to restore them, but inevitably often to see and accompany them safely through 'the veil' before themselves returning to this familiar world we call life as though there were no other. That ill-reputed star and degree showed them a view that few of us are privileged to know.

The author, Kim's husband for her last few days of mortal life, has his own Lilith opposite to her Sun in Neptune, and in his 12th house.

In summary, the two *Scales*, like **Libra** itself, are symbolic of all that we find most difficult to come to terms with, and that above all because we still know so little of ourselves, either singly or collectively, our past history and its scars left upon us, and therefore who and what we truly are today. If **Scorpio**, to which we come next, but which has already figured so strongly in our pages, is the Sign and Constellation that calls us to dig deep and investigate the unknown, then **Libra** is that first shock discovery that, whatever we may find ourselves to be, it isn't what hitherto we have comfortably but illusorily thought ourselves to be.

CHAPTER 12

Scorpio the Scorpion

The Constellation and Sign of **Scorpio** is undoubtedly one of the most colourful characters in the entire heavens, in or out of the Zodiac. The name is sometimes spelt *Scorpius*, not a mistake in our latin but telling us that this is one particular scorpion, not just any example of that species.

In Greek mythology, it is the scorpion which the goddess Juno, wife of Jupiter and mother-figure to the world of living creatures, sent to sting the hunter Orion as he was about to slay Taurus the bull. In our night sky **Scorpio** is opposite to **Orion** and **Taurus**, but with the Hunter lower than the Bull, so that as the Scorpion rises, the Hunter sets, leaving the Bull safely alone there.

All this has a lot to do with the historical evolution of human culture, marking the change from the nomadic 'kill-eat-move on' mode of life in the Aries era to the settled farming civilisation of Taurus, so that it was this development that Juno was protecting.

It was then that the Bull became a major cult object of

worship, which Moses had to contend against at the time for moving humanity on into the Gemini era of humanity's rise to learning and developing the intellect above the simple agricultural plane.

This astrological way of mapping human development is of course grossly over simplified, for it shows up the situation in certain advanced communities rather than in humanity as a whole, some sections of which are even today still climbing painfully out of eras that others have left far behind them.

And one can read the progression in the opposite direction through the Zodiac, where Taurus represents the development of communal life, the group mode under a chieftain, akin to the herd of cows dominated by a single bull. This sprang from the Gemini era in which loyalties were limited to the single partner with whom one mated, as the pair of humans in that Sign, one of each sex, is often portrayed in both astrology and tarot. After Taurus then came Aries the Sign of aggression, conquest and new beginnings, when the apostles of the new way of life spread their civilisations and imposed them on others by force of arms.

Returning to (**Scorpio**), now considering it as an astrological Sign, it is the eighth one of the Zodiac and, like the eighth house of the horoscope, it is very much about profound and irreversible changes in the life pattern: as a house, for the individual; as a Sign, for life as a whole. After what we saw of 19° (**Scorpio**) in the previous chapter, we can appreciate that it signifies the most profound change that ever happened to us, through the explosion or 'Fall' of Phaethon.

It is no surprise, therefore, that, in some cultures, notably Chinese, this Sign is seen as a *Dragon*, the fire-breathing monster with the long tail. All the ancient records of that event describe it as a huge tail of fire in the sky, swinging towards Earth with the threat of cooking us completely, just as would always be seen between binary stars in the imminence of one of them exploding, only to be stopped short of total disaster when the doomed star finally disintegrated. In some romantic tellings, Jupiter hit Phaethon with a thunderbolt to save us; in others, the Dragon was slain by a St. George type of hero; in others the Dragon itself swallowed up the errant star. Thus dragons are much feared in some cultures, highly regarded as lucky in others. The barbed or arrowheaded tail so often portrayed on dragons (and on Satan, our adversary), implying that it stings with it, brings us back to the Scorpion theme again, which really does attack in that way.

We have dealt often enough now with the immense evolutionary impact of the 'Fall of Phaethon' that we need not labour it again. The connection with the eighth house of astrology, with death and resurgence in a new state, is now quite obvious in Scorpio. And it is for this reason that it is also seen sometimes as the Sign of the *Phoenix*, the mythical bird which emerges anew from being consumed by fire. Sir William Drummond held that the patriach Abraham regarded this Sign as the *Eagle*, while others have seen it as Noah's *Dove*, both of them ancient symbols of resurgence but probably in both cases the substitution of a real and familiar bird for the mythical symbol. Some cultures, notably Aztec and Maya, have portrayed a *Snake* here, again a real animal in place of the symbolic *Dragon*.

Finally in introducing **Scorpio**, there is the problem that in many old cultures this creature was not distinguished from the Crab, which of course we already have in the Zodiac as **Cancer**. Even well into the Middle Ages of our own era, some quite learned people still believed that crabs were the progenitors of scorpions! So we shall find that error reflected in some of the star names that now follow. Modern Arabic has the word Sartaan for a crab, but Aqrab for scorpion, and that once meant both of these creatures.

The prime star of **Scorpio** is *Antares*, a name meaning 'Rival to Mars'. Classified as α Scorpio, it is a 'red giant' of some 350 million miles diameter (560 km) so that if it were where our Sun is, we should be deep inside it, and planet Mars would be skimming closely round its surface. In the night sky it is often more visible than Mars itself, and easily mistaken for the planet if their positions be close at the time of observing. Currently *Antares* is 9°40' of (**Sagittarius**), which is 16° of **Scorpio**, almost the centre of the Constellation. It thus deserves well its other main title: Heart of the Scorpion, Cor Scorpionis, Kardia Skorpion (Καρδια Σκορπιον), Qalb Al Aqrab, according to your linguistic tastes.

There have been other titles, however, apart from the same name in other tongues of course. It has been called 'Antar's star', and the Antar there referred to may have been the legendary giant Anteus, a reference to the star's hugh size. But the Antar may also have been Antarah, the Arab-Negro military leader in Mecca just before the rise of Islam. Equally, that man may have adopted the name of the great war star as his revolutionary pseudonym as such people still adopt symbolic names today. (Lenin- Light; Stalin- Steel; Molotov-Hammer). In China it has been Hwo Sing, Fire Star; in Babylon it was Urbat in the asterism Hurru, Divine Protector.

The Babylonian title brings us to this star's role as one of the four Archangel stars: *Fomalhaut* – Gabriel, *Aldebaran* – Michael, *Regulus* – Raphael, and now *Antares* – Uriel. The City of Ur, where Abraham was born, is said to have been the first city to be build after the Great Disaster, and was given the name of Earth itself: Urs. That city stood close to the site of later Babylon itself, not too far from modern Baghdad. Uriel, the Archangel not mentioned in the sacred texts made available to the public, was the one who held the secret knowledge of that Great Disaster, and only revealed it to those judged able to accept it and still believe in the Divine Goodness in all that befalls us. Again this is all so very **Scorpio** in nature than one cannot miss or deride its ring of truth.

Ptolemy classified *Antares* as a Mars-Jupiter type, and all astrologers have noted it as an indicator of success in war, and high command therein, but not forgetting that one's opponent may well have the support of *Aldebaran*, the star opposite to this one, and star of Archangel Michael, commander of the Heavenly Host itself! What does tend to show up when these two stars are both engaged on the horoscope of a conflict, either the starting date of the war, or the natal charts of the leaders, is that peace rarely ensues before the total and crushing defeat of one side or the other. And it is a war that escalates to huge proportions, even to a world scale, as aggressive Mars in precedence over expansive Jupiter would imply.

But war is not the only outlet for the symbolism of *Antares*, and it indicates just as often the individual's great store of energy and optimism to undertake ventures which others could not attempt.

According to the planets involved, and the house on the horoscope where *Antares* is found, such ventures can include anything from sports achievements and exploration of antarctica or the Moon, to diplomacy of the most hazardous kind or scientific research at the extremes of human knowledge and ability.

Having dealt thus far with **Scorpio's** major and central star, we go now to the earliest one in the constellation as it now stands, which is δ Scorpii at 2°20' of (**Sagittarius**), 8°39' of **Scorpio**. Some lists name it as *Aqrab* (Q is pronounced like K, by the way) but this is almost useless to us, that word meaning only 'scorpion', and the same is sometimes applied to the lesser stars of **Libra** also, those which have not been worth our while to mention.

δ Scorpii is better named as either *Isidis* or *Dschubba*. The origins of both names are obscure but the first probably connects with the Egyptian goddess Isis; the second looks like a pretty amateurish germanic corruption of Al Jabbah, the Forehead, which is where we find it on the Scorpion. Since that name has already been used for a star in the forehead of **Leo**, we shall do better to keep it here as *Dschubba*, the clumsy spelling notwithstanding. The Babylonian title Qabu sha Rishu Aqrabi, Centre of the Head of the Scorpion, confirms our 'guess' at the Arabic title before it was transliterated by Herr Somebody, but a still earlier

Mesopotamian culture had it as Jia Jan Ju Sur, which seems to have meant the forbidden Tree of Life in Eden. So again we find this Constellation luring us back to look at our origins as a species of living creature.

Ptolemy classes it as a Mars-Saturn star, not a very delightful combination, yet one which makes certain sense when we remember that a scorpion's armament is at the rear, not in the head where this star is. It is in fact a fighter of very great skill, and that characterises Mars-Saturn perfectly. Anyone with *Dschubba* strong on the horoscope is likely to show a patient and wary approach to any situations, but this will belie the skilled determination which will then be brought to bear. **Scorpio** is famous for the surgeons born in it and this star shows up just the qualities which they need to have. The same applies to generals, policemen, private investigators and secret service agents, many of whom have *Dschubba* well placed and aspected. In research of all other kinds too, it distinguishes the real adept.

Next we find *Graffias*, β Scorpii, in some past time the second brightest in the Constellation, although the previous entry, δ, now outshines it by a little. *Graffias* is currently at 3°3' (**Sagittarius**), 9°22' **Scorpio**, and the name almost certainly comes from Υραψαιos, the psi in the middle of Grapsaios having been mistaken for phi at some time. The word means simply 'crab', again showing the confusion of the two creatures in the past. Use of the Arabic Aqrab, as in some modern lists, should be avoided, as already explained, even though it refers to the right creature. It is another Mars-Saturn star in Ptolemy and, close as it is to *Dschuba*, the two may be regarded effectively as one unit. Together with two or three other minor stars very close by, they were known collectively as *Al Iklil* (or *Al Yukallil*) *Al Jabbah*, the Crown of, or on, the Forehead (of the Scorpion), and just about the only part of this Sign or Constellation to have been regarded as auspicious.

Lesath is our next star, υ Scorpio, at 23°50' (**Sagittarius**), and now at 0°9' **Sagittarius** by sidereal reckoning. Nonetheless it must be regarded still as a **Scorpio** star that has now modified its earlier meaning for us, just as has the Leo star Regulus since coming so close to (**Virgo**), and the Virgo star Khambalia now in (**Scorpio**) and **Libra**.

The name, sometimes written *Lesuth*, means Sting, derived from the Arabic *Al Lathagh* or, earlier, *Al Las'ah*. Another name seen occasionally is *Al Fikrah* but this has been applied to each of the string of stars marking the vertebrae of the long tail, whereas the one now under discussion truly is the one at the tip, and is thus the sting. Not unexpectedly it gets a Mercury-Mars rating from Ptolemy, what else for a deft and swift injector like this?

Its qualities in the horoscope are very much those of a probing, sharp intellect and an incisive wit, every bit as damaging as a knife to an opponent, but more confined now to the intellectual level than in times when it did not have so much of a Sagittarian quality. It is one of three **Scorpio** stars which can be held to account for the often surprising bite in otherwise genial, jovial (**Sagittarians**), but it does show them to have an enterprising spirit of keenness of insight not always thought of in connection with that religio-philosophical ninth Sign of the Zodiac. People with this star strong on their charts are noted for doing well in debate, business, sport, and high office in general. If not well aspected, though, they can be inclined to strike first and ask afterwards, with an embarrassing loss of face.

Close after that star we have the redoubtable *Aculeus* at 25°44' (**Sagittarius**), 2°3' in the same by Sidereal accounting, but still a **Scorpio** item, and then we have *Acumen* at 28°44' and 4°53′ respectively. Both of these are multiple clusters, not single stars, *Aculeus* being M6 in the Messier catalogue, while *Acumen* is M7. They are of immense size, as comparable to galaxies as to stars, but very far distant and very faint, when visible at all to the eye. Ptolemy listed them both as Mars-Moon stars, probably unaware that they were clusters, and both names echo the previous entry, meaning Sting.

Both have a notorious reputation in astrology as 'Blind Stars' and are said to inflict blindness for certain on the one unlucky in having them prominent on the horoscope. Leaving aside the suggestion that any star 'inflicts' anything at all, yes, the author has found that people with these and/or the other 'blind stars' prominent do have eyesight problems, but then so has he, and he does not have them prominent on his own chart.

But he has noted a number of cases of clients asking his advice about forthcoming eye treatment, especially operations, and showing excessive worry about the outcome, unaware that one or other of these stars really was going to be strong on their charts on the date in question. It does no harm at all then to advise the client to seek another date, or a second medical opinion, if only because their nervousness may communicate itself to the surgeon and actually precipitate an error in that way. Beyond that, one must allow that the presence of the stars upon the event may indeed be a sign that the client has indeed premonitored an unfortunate outcome, by whatever mode of intuition may be working within him or her.

In the narrow longitudinal space between *Aculeus* and *Acumen* is the star *Etamin*, α Draconis, chief star and one of the eyes of *Draco* the Dragon Constellation, and it may well be that it was this one which caused the other two to be so much associated with eyesight. But *Etamin* seems not to have been noted by Ptolomy. It is currently at 27°4' (**Sagittarius**), 4°1' sidereally.

Apart from that ominous portent, these two star clusters do show up a negative Mars-Moon quality in people who have them poorly aspected, with a tendency towards a morbid outlook, seeing the worst rather than the best in everything. If their religious views are affected, as so often with anything in (**Sagittarius**), there is the tendency to be either of the 'hellfire and damnation brigade' or to take up a fierce anti-religious and even an anti-God stance. But at their best, well aspected, they can have very sharp minds and a perception well above average as though, perhaps 'blind' to what we see and take for granted, they see what we do not, at levels where eyesight does not reach. Not for nothing has the word *Acumen* come down to us as a term for a very sharp mind.

There are many more stars in **Scorpio**, a large constellation which extends far over the sky and both north and south of our Equator. The majority of the remaining stars are in the tail which has already received so much of our attenion, and so do not really add anything new to what we have now said. Knowing when to stop is an essential part of reading the meaning of the vast families of stars that surround us, or we risk overloading our minds for no better purpose than to quote a lot of names. And so we leave **Scorpio** as we have now seen it.

CHAPTER 13

Sagittarius the Archer

Once upon a time, so mythology tells us, there was a large herd of strange creatures whose body and hind legs were those of a horse but whose portion from the shoulders upward was the torso and head and arms of a man. By some accounts the creature also had the forelegs of a horse, making the animal six-limbed in all, but other portrayals omit the forelegs, leaving us to wonder how this creature balanced and ran with its extraordinary speed and power. These creatures, called Centaurs, were a wild and unruly tribe, and thoroughly dangerous with the bows and arrows they always carried, but were much beloved of Jupiter, who of course had created them.

That story is too much for even the most far-fetched imagination in genetic hybrid engineering, and we must seek other explanations for it having originated in the human mind. One idea commonly put forward is that certain tribes of humans who had not tamed the horse and learned to ride it were attacked by cavalry from elsewhere and, in their terror, genuinely thought horse and rider to be one creature.

That seems too likely not to be true, and we can imagine the victims of the attack, a simple people whose means of transport when not on foot was the slowly plodding ox, describing their attackers as having 'the power of a hundred bulls' – cent-tauri, as we now have it in Latin. But if that very exoteric answer is the right answer, then we have here a case of 'introjection' as psychology likes to say: we took an external phenomenon and made of it an inner, esoteric symbol. The human is a comparatively weak animal for its size – even a medium dog can give us a rough time of it – and so the idea of having a much greater strength latent within us must have had an immense appeal. Do we not compare those we admire with the lion, or those we despise for their brute clumsiness with the bull (in a china shop)?

But the horse has a special place in our affections, since we have derived so much of our mastery of the world from having learned to ride it, have it pull our wagons and plough our fields, and make fortunes for us on the race-track (if we own it, or make the book!). No other animal, not even the most endangered species, commands prices like those paid for a good horse. Its manifest intelligence too has long earned our respect.

And then springs the feeling that, could we but really find our way inwards to the Creator Who made both the horse and ourselves, then all would be well for us, for He is the source of boundless strength and intelligence and all else we could need. We are that Centaur if we can but find our Centre. The pun is intentional, and not flippant, for it is well known that our subliminal consciousness knows and uses that 'language of the gods' quite seriously.

Yet we are often very fearful of the vast power latent there, for in truth we doubt our capacity to handle it safely, and people who become either religious maniacs or megalomaniacs are warning enough of the havoc it can wreak if we fail to control what we unleash there. So the Centaurs are seen as a wild, unruly bunch, all save one of them, the centaur Chiron. Driven out of the herd as 'a prophet not wanted in his own country', mortally wounded but not able to die, this one centaur went forth to teach and uplift humanity until that species should be fit to sit at the foot of the Divine Throne, no less.

Just how many stories we now have of such a prophet, or messiah, or avatar coming amongst us by Divine Command is all but past counting, but it is surely no accident that the early Christians adopted the Greek letters 'χρ', Chiro, as their sacred glyph for the new faith. And, of course, there are all the necessary trappings to the story: non-acceptance by his own people, mortally wounded by them, resurrected from death, and, beyond any sound dispute at all, a teacher of the most immense importance to humanity, whose message has been far from exhausted, or even fully grasped, even 1900 years after him.

So we see how **Sagittarius** symbolises all that is greatest in Life and in our prospects in that life. There is the power theme there, of the herd of Centaurs, so we associate it with great athletic and adventure achievements, and big business. There is the finding of the Divinity there, so it is also the Sign of religion, philosophy, Creation, and God (to Whom be Praise). There also is the eternal Avatar, Prophet, Messiah, Christ who comes periodically to lead us another step along our way to the Life Eternal.

There is, in the southern hemisphere of our skies, another constellation of the same symbol, actually named **Centaurus**, larger in fact than the one we are now dicussing, and some commentators have wanted to associate **Centaurus** rather than **Sagittarius** with Chiron. Of course it must be so associated, as we shall see later, but it is not necessary to set the two Constellations up as rivals like this. Perhaps we should see the existence of two complementary figures, one north, one south, as manifesting the Great Teaching throughout the world. But for now we go on with **Sagittarius**.

The first 'star' we come to is in fact the massive *Trifid Nebula*, listed by Messier as at least three separate but close clusters,

M8, M20 and M21, and taking its name from its appearance in the telescope as a huge plant of the tradescantia type. It is well worth a look if even a modest telescope is available. In astrology it goes by the name also *Spiculum*, latin for Dart, or point of an arrow or similar weapon.

Its current position is 0°30' **(Capricorn)**, 6°49' **Sagittarius**, very close to the estimated position for the centre of our Galaxy, and thus especially symbolising for us the prime point of the Creation. (Other reckonings in astrology give 15° **(Capricorn)** for this 'Centre of the Universe.'

Ptolemy rates *Spiculum* as a Mars-Moon type, another of the 'blind stars' and a figure of great foreboding. We must at least go along with the planetary simile, for there is indeed a strong tendency towards depression and a rather morbid outlook religiously in horoscopes having this star strong and harshly aspected on them. Such a condition does of itself make for all manner of problems, of course, psychological and physical, eyesight included. There is often that feeling of negative 'fear of God', rather than comfort from the sensing of His Presence, the feeling that He is Omnipotent in such a way that the individual's life is of no concern to Him, so that we are hopelessly doomed. The classic novel *The day of the Trifids*, with its fear of extinction of humanity by mere plants, conveys the negative associations of this nebula perfectly.

But well aspected, the *Trifid*, or *Spiculum*, shows just the opposite in the person. There can be a very real feel of companionship with the entire Universe and its Creator, and a remarkable ability to plunge deeply into the seas of philosophy and come up with joyous and meaningful answers through a very happy intuition. The author, having this one right on his seventh house cusp, is especially sensitive to it, and could write volumes (but will spare you from them) on the alternations of seemingly colossal responsibility, when he is a bit under par, but of immense resource for recovery just by asking for it, from that Source to which he is as physically blind as everyone else.

The two prime stars of **Sagittarius** astronomically speaking, α and β, do not figure often in astrology; for one thing, they are not in fact the brighest, or even second brightest in the constellation, and also they are so close in longitude to other stars which are used.

But they deserve a mention just the same, *Rukbat Al Rami*, the name of α Sagittarii, means Knee of the Archer. Sometimes the first word is left off, so the meaning then is just The Archer. To see it as the knee, one must draw the Archer as a fully human figure kneeling to take aim, as later artists have sometimes drawn it. The Chaldean title *Nibat Anu*, probably meaning a chief star, is also used sometimes. The position by longitude is almost the same as *Manubrium* (coming soon) but α is well to the south of it.

β Sagittarii is in fact a pair of stars, only close to each other as seen from Earth, and usually go by the name *Arkab*, or *Urkub*, or *Al Urkhub*, all meaning the tendon in the leg just above the ankle, in either man or horse. The Chaldean name *Ur Ner Gub* means Sole of the Foot. The Arab astronomer Kazwini called the pair *Al Suradaïin*, The Two Plovers, seemingly nothing to do with **Sagittarius** as we know it. These two stars are close to *Vega* (α Lyrae) in longitude, but again very far south of it, being in fact the southernmost stars in their own figure.

A star which concerns us very much, and the next in longitude after *Spiculum* with which we began, is *Polis*, μ Sagittarii, currently at 3°6' **(Capricorn)**, 8°38' **Sagittarius**. It is in fact a group of four stars, only close by appearance, three of them known as μ_1, the other, a little away from those, being μ_2. The name is not the Greek for a town, as might be thought, but Coptic for a Foal. It may be that it was this star that Omar Khayyam referred to when he wrote:

> I tell you this; when starting from the Goal,
> Over the shoulders of the flaming Foal
> Of Heaven, Parw'in and Mushtara they flung
> In my predestined Plot of Dust and Soul

That name does not sound much connected with our Archer, and may once have not been included, for it lies at the far northern tip of his bow, beyond the star named as its north marker (our next entry).

For all that, this Jupiter-Mars star as Ptolemy has it, shows up in a horoscope with almost the regal qualities of mighty *Regulus*. Only *Polis* will indicate more of the high office in spiritual life, Pope, Imam, Archbishop, or at least a prominent Theologian, than in the temporal world of kings and statesmen. Unfavourably aspected, however, it may show more the self-styled pretender to such dignity, or the one who on gaining appointment fails to meet expectations. If better than that by aspect, but not aided by Sun or tenth house, say, then we still have someone whose interest and knowledge of things spiritual may be both keen and profound.

Kaus Borealis, λ Sagittarii, is currently at 6°9′ **(Capricorn)**, 11°41′ **Sagittarius**, and is a hybrid of Arabic and Latin, coming from *Al Qaus Al Shamali*, the Northern (star in the) Bow. At some earlier time, this and several other stars near it were associated with keeping Ostriches, of which there seemed to be a herd in this part of the sky (perhaps on the ground too), and the names *Al Rais Al Na'ams* or *Al Thalimain* still turn up in some literature. But the Archer and his bow are now firmly established, so we stick with *Kaus Borealis* for our purposes here. Ptolemy does not appear to have included this star, having so many to choose from in this Constellation, but if he had then he could well have classed it as a Mercury-Mars type. It does convey a sense of strength and flexibility combined and this often shows up in the horoscopes of people who can put great force behind their reasoning, yet be somewhat more flexible than those we have just described under *Polis*. Much the same applies to *Kaus Meridionalis (Al Qaus Al Wasat)*, δ Sagittarii, in the Middle of the Bow, and to *Kaus Australis (Al Qaus Al Janubi)*, ε Sagittarii, in the Southern part. The latter is practically conjunct in longitude with Kaus Borealis, while the Middle one lies just back a little towards *Polis*. Hardly more than 3° separates the whole four of them.

Now again we come to a really major one, famous or

notorious as you will, but certainly much talked of in astrology, and another of those clusters which **Sagittarius** has in plenty, Messier's M22, its name *Facies*, its current positions 8°14' **(Capricorn)**, 13°46' **Sagittarius**. Ptolemy rates it as Sun-Mars; it is another 'blind star' and much blamed also for accidents with broken limbs and so-on. The Latin name is from the verb Facere, to make or do something, and it is often said to portend accidents due to the victim's own careless actions.

Naturally there is a positive side to *Facies*, even if rarely given space in the works of the gloom mongers. It symbolises well that kind of Sagittarian who goes out to climb mountains, race cars, enter the ski-jump team or the Grand National steeplechase, making it right to the top and no doubt breaking a few bones at times along the way. If he is Sagittarian by Sun-sign, he will have this star in his solar first or second house, with consequent physical effect upon him for good or ill, depending upon what aspects and conjuncts it has. On the more philosophical side it will mark those who must see their outlook and beliefs carried into practical effect somewhere, so that they go out on missions, set up their own churches and centres, engage in good works of famine or refugee relief, and so on. Inevitably they get hurt at times, but perhaps find compensation in the value of their works.

Pelagus, alias *Nunki* is σ Sagittarii, at the rear end of the arrow in the Archer's bow, and we find it now at 12°12' **(Capricorn)**. 17°44' **Sagittarius**. Ptolemy classes it as a Jupiter-Mercury star and, with a Vis.Mag, of 2.14, it is one of the brightest in this generally rather faint Constellation. The Latin name, given first here, means the Open Sea, while *Nunki* is a word of Chaldean roots, all that is left to us from a longer expression: 'The Edict of the Sea.' When we come to **Pisces** we shall find another star, *Kullat Nuni*, with very similar connotation, but perhaps more to be expected there in the watery Constellation of the fishes.

The immense and inexorable power of the sea has always impressed humanity with a sense of the Divine Power which alone can rule such a force, and the idea of the Divinity commanding it is well suggested by both the 'Edict' title and the 'God is speaking' theme in Ptolemy's planetary simile for this star. *Pelagus, Nunki*, is therefore an indicator on the chart of one who may be expected to be quite the authoritative orator on any matters concerned with the topics of **Sagittarius** and **(Capricorn)**: Religion, Business, State and Foreign Affairs. Interest in long-distance travel and the ships and airplanes that make it possible is also likely, and it is interesting that the famous but very reclusive entrepreneur Howard Hughes had Phaethon on this star, a situation akin to having the visible Sun there but without the wish for publicity, even a desire to avoid it. An air-hostess friend of the author has her lunar South Node on *Nunki*, and Lilith on the North Node opposite: while happy and successful in her job, she also feels a keen calling to religion and spiritual healing.

Ascella, or *Axilla*, ζ Sagittarii, is the Latin name for the armpit of the Archer, which is where this star is located. Presently at 13°27' **(Capricorn)**, 19° **Sagittarius**, it is within the orb of both the preceding star *Pelagus*, and the next one, *Manubrium*, and indeed the very bright *Vega* (α Lyrae) next after that, and which may be said by some to dominate the whole group here. We shall see more of *Vega* later. Each must be seen as adding qualities to the others, and receiving the same from them. *Ascella* needs little further comment from us since, being another Jupiter-Mercury type it really serves simply to widen the orb of *Pelagus*.

Manubrium, o Sagittarii, is in fact another globular cluster, and thus registered also as Messier's M55. It is now at 14°52' **(Capricorn)** or 20°24' **Sagittarius**, and the name means a *handle*. Possibly this comes from some sketches of the Archer in which the hand holding the string of the bow is pulled right back to the position of this star. It is a Sun-Mars type, by Ptolemy, and must thus be considered another of the 'blind stars'. But the same planetary simile is of course symbolic of the fatal potency in the hand that may at any moment release the arrow into flight. To find a major planet in a horoscope very precisely on *Manubrium* rather than its neighbours is likely to show up the more aggressive connotations of the Constellation and Sign here, and we should often find less of the philosopher than the high-performance athlete or, bearing in mind the juridical associations of the ninth and tenth regions of the Zodiac, the high-court judge. The military strategist is also likely to have this star strong.

Terebellum, ω Sagittarii, is the last of our stars in the Archer, at 25°44' **(Capricorn)**, 1°16' **Capricorn**, having thus advanced sidereally from its home Constellation into the next, with consequent modification of its significance in earlier times. The name of this Venus-Saturn star does not spring from the Latin 'Bellum', War, but from Ptolemy's Greek name for it, τετραπλερου, a quadrangle, for it is in fact a close group of four stars on the hip of the horse body of **Sagittarius**. This is, of course, a muscular part from which a horse draws much of its strength and thus its potential for becoming a great winner.

We are not surprised therefore that, 'in the background' though the position may at first seem to be, it often does reveal the potential which people have to become leading figures in their field of work or their community. If well aspected on their charts, it shows them able to wield much power and authority with a venusian ease and attractiveness that keeps them secure in their position. If negatively aspected or conjunct with Saturn or Mars, however, we may instead find them at the mercy of authority against which they can effectively do nothing to help themselves. In such a situation they do well to avoid the scramble for power and position, for they may still do much good to themselves and others by offering quietly and gently the wisdom which they undoubtedly hold within.

Sagittarius, taken overall, is a marker in the Heavens showing us where we may find great support from our inborn facility for communion with all that is Divine and can inspire us, but that does of itself impose a responsibility to use wisely what we thus receive. One does not set the moron loose among the complexities of a power-station.

CHAPTER 14

Capricorn the Sea-Goat

Quite often one sees this tenth Constellation and Sign of the Zodiac described as 'The Goat', but it is correctly the 'Sea-Goat', a creature of subjective mythology rather than everyday zoology.

An exhausting plough through volumes of written material on this animal very nearly fails to produce anything intelligible, yet there are just one or two pointers to its history, of which an ancient tale from the Far East seems the most helpful. **Capricorn** in that account was an amphibious figure of some ill-defined kind but significant for being the nurse, and thus female, to the young Sun god.

This story is so old, predating by far the Greek myth of Amalthea as nurse to the infant Jupiter, that it must go back to the dawn of the revival of life after the Great Disaster which left us with only one sun instead of two. The date of that disaster is known with fair certainty, Otto von Muck's 8498 BC perhaps a little over preicse, but seeingly right within a year or two. Less easy to state for sure is the ensuing period during which all sunlight was blotted out by thick dust clouds over most of the planet. Estimates vary between 1500 and 3000 years.

Taking 19° **Scorpio** as the point at which the Earth was struck, and the daylight blotted out, a period of 2406 years would see the whole Zodiac pass us by for one circuit (2160 years, a 'Great Year'), then 246 years to carry us from the Disaster degree to 0° **Capricorn**, and the reappearance of sunlight. But it would be a quite different scene from what had been known before, and which had been handed down through the generations of survivors, 'the people that walked in darkness' – *Isaiah*. So that when 'they saw the Great Light' *(ibid)* it would be as a new Sun, or a young Sun-god, and **Capricorn** the nurse that brought it into the world.

Anything new or seemingly new on the cosmic scale is inevitably compared with the vastness of the ocean and, since on this occasion it brought light to the people on land, the half fish/half animal image of the Sea-Goat seems natural enough.

The choice of goat for the animal part of the symbol is itself interesting in view of the distinction made between goats and sheep in many esoteric and religious literary works. Zoologically, they are almost identical creatures, but the sheep is regarded as a docile, obedient and unquestioning follower of the shepherd (only if he is carrying a sack of feed for them – this author's personal experience!), whereas the goat has a mind of its own and an intellect that the goatherd must learn to negotiate with.

This is, no doubt, how the goat came to be the symbol of both Pan and Satan and how those in turn became the patrons of the cults which opposed the unquestioning sheep-like obedience and suppression of any goat-like individual initiative or intelligence, which was demanded by the church establishments from the 4th Century A.D. onwards. The goat, in any of its god-like forms, instructs or tempts Man (according to our point of view) to use his own intelligence and willpower against that of God, or the establishments which claim to speak for Him (again according to our view of the matter). And the ruling planet of **Capricorn** is of course Saturn, alias Satan or Pan.

A couple more notes are worth making on the 'sea-animal' nature of this creature. Some commentators have found evidence of it being connected in certain cultures with the swordfish, others with the narwhal, both of them sea creatures with a horn, loosely interpreting that for the sharp nose of one, the tusk of the other, and the narwhal is quite certainly an animal (not fish) of the whale family. This may be nothing better than a latterday rationalisation, however. Secondly, there are others who have suggested more cogently that some of the survivors of the Disaster may have spent two and a half millennia at sea in the less afflicted parts of the world, perhaps where thinner cloud allowed at least some amount of hazy light to penetrate, before making permanent landfall when the Sun was seen again.

In that case the intelligent sea-animal **Capricorn** is humanity itself, and so we explain a very early Hindu term for it as 'The Double Ship'. A very old Persian-Gulf (Chaldean or earlier) name for it was 'Father of Light', which again speaks of the 'new' Sun appearing first in this Constellation. All this allegory of the rebirth of civilisation and human power gives us new understanding of **Capricorn** as also the 'House of Kings' and any auspicious item in this Sign or the Tenth House on a horoscope indicating potential power for the individual over communities of people.

Finally, in the context of the return of the Sun, **Capricorn** is of course the Sun-sign of the Winter Solstice, when the Sun has reached its lowest declination and then begins its climb back into our view again. But that would only explain a term like 'Father of Light' if that had been an Eskimo term, not one used in the Arabian Sea, where the daylight remains considerable, even in midwinter. And it certainly does not explain how such a strange animal image came to be associated with it. Now we shall turn our attention to its major stars.

Giedi is the first star by longitude in **Capricorn**, also the first by Greek letter rating, α Capricorni, though not actually the brightest. It should be pronounced 'zhaydy', coming from one of the Arabic words for a goat: *Al Jadii*. The present position is 3°39' **(Aquarius)**, 9°11' **Capricorn**. Situated in the head of the creature, it is actually a stellium of five stars in two very close groups, α_1 and α_2. The first contains three stars, the second two. Very close to these is γ Capricorni, *Al Shat* (the Sheep), generally viewed as a 'sacrificial lamb' symbol, while conjunct in longitude but somewhat to the south of the others is β Capricorni, *Dabih*, 'The Slaughterer'. This is another apparent double star, β_1 and β_2 currently at 3°53' **(Aquarius)**, 9°25' **Capricorn**. It will serve us best to consider this whole group at once.

Ptolemy gave *Giedi* the very unusual rating of a Venus-Mars type, while *Dabih*, its full name being Al Sa'ad al Dhabih, the Lucky Slaughterer, is a Saturn-Venus. He did not mention *Al Shat*, which seems to have been introduced into the scene by Arab astronomers, for the attention of Mr. Dabih, we must presume.

Readers will generally be familiar with the story of Abraham being spared at the last moment from having to sacrifice his son Isaac when God provided a sheep as an alternative. Learned clergy of three religions have written volumes about this legend, a rather sick one to most people today. Human sacrifice may have had its origins in one of two ways after the Great Disaster: either the shortage of food was such that warring between communities was conducted for what little was available, including the bodies captured, dead or alive, or else the general condition of the survivors was so poor that the leaders had many of them culled to preserve the quality of the fitter ones. It sounds horrible either way, and so it was, but quite possible. The growth of the idea that it was Divinely ordained is not surprising in the wake of a cosmic disaster that had almost wiped out everyone.

Abraham broke with his community in Ur, putting his trust totally in God as he went into the lifeless desert, where no-one would have expected him to survive any time at all, and after a while he may well have come to the pass where his tiny group must perish without the sacrifice of one of them. Even the great Patriarch seemed to be forced back to the ways he had left behind him, and one telling of the story has it that he was praying for his own sudden death as he raised the knife, if no other miracle was to be forthcoming.

The miracle happened in the form of a ram, and the 'Lucky Slaughterer' got the message at once. Human sacrifice was to be no more: God had clearly said it. The 'Tenth Sign', **Capricorn**, may here be seen as both God and Abraham, the Venus-Mars simile as a new order in peace and war, a new covenant between human needs and the means of obtaining them, while the Saturn-Venus simile surely must be God restraining the hand of the man-of-peace to spare him from his most horrible act of necessity. This seems to be all the more apposite today, with these stars now in the 'humanitarian' Sign of **(Aquarius)**.

So what we should expect from *Giedi* and *Dabih* strong in a horoscope is that the person having them there will show great patience and trust, Faith, in a crisis, yet with a decisiveness that will take action as needed, not fudge the issue. Of course that means that such people are likely to meet with crises in plenty and, if the aspects be harsh ones, more crises than anyone would wish.

If Saturn or Mars be among the planets thus involved, the strain upon the person may be too much in the end, but the benefics, Jupiter and Venus, will show such a person to be a seemingly inexhaustible tower of strength to others in difficult times. 'Buzz' Aldrin, of Moon landing fame, has Mercury here, with Sun just before it on star *Altair* (α Aquilae, q.v), and both in trine aspect to Jupiter in his twelfth house, just the man-of-faith one would wish for in such a venture.

The intrepid aviatrix of the 1930s Amelia Earhart, had Midheaven here, but Sun opposite, suggesting possibly one venture too many at the end. The courageous French novelist and radical Victor Hugo had Mars here, and by the bye, the present author has noted at least six astrologers (himself not included) to have strong items here. They all worked with faith in their art when it was generally ridiculed and even invited prosecution in court.

Oculus and *Bos*, π and ρ Capricorni respectively, are our next pair, only 28' apart, centred at 4°48' **(Aquarius)**, 10°20' **Capricorn**.

The first name is Latin for Eye, its position in the figure, while Bos means Ox. It is a little curious that this name turns up in Latin, for it is only known otherwise in that way as the Chinese asterism Kien Niew (Ox). Ptolemy, sensibly considering these two stars as effectively one, rated them as of the nature of Saturn-Venus, so that they virtually extend the range of *Dabih* before them. But they are that bit further from *Giedi*, so there is less of martian quality.

Horoscopes with these well aspected, therefore, will show an ease of command in state, church or business, but with a tendency towards conservatism, and perhaps a lack of forward-looking vision in time of crisis. Herbert Hoover, leading U.S. statesman at the time of the Wall Street financial crash, 1930, had his Midheaven here, while his successor, Franklin Roosevelt, had Sun on the more aggressive and progressive Mars-Mercury star *Armus*, our next entry.

Yes, *Armus*, η Capricorni, is at 12°36' **(Aquarius)**, 18°8' **Capricorn**, and the name (Latin) means Shoulder, its position in the figure. As has just been said, it is a Mars-Mercury type by Ptolemy. Like all the **Capricorn-(Aquarius)** stars, it features prominently with those people who engage in statesmanship, politics, religious and humanitarian causes, and this includes the kind of author and poet who consciously writes with the social impact of his work in mind. After the steady falling-off of initiative, from *Giedi* (or really from *Altair* before it) to *Bos*, we find *Armus* returning to the fray with great vigour. The example of F.D. Roosevelt has been mentioned and, tame though his policies may seem to us now, they really were a martian attack on the monetary (mercury) system in his day, with courageous vision there. The image of the Shoulder symbolises well the willingness of *Armus* people to 'shoulder the burden' at times of crises. Charles de Gaulle, who 'picked up the pieces' twice in recent French history when others had given up and he himself had little more than words left to fight with, had Mars on *Armus*, as well as his Ascendant on *Giedi*.

Our next star, *Dorsum*, θ Capricorni, is close enough in longitude to *Armus* that one may consider them as an astrological pair, if an item on the horoscope lies between them, but the distance is sufficient to take each of them alone, if the item lies just before the first or just after the second.

Dorsum, meaning The Back, is on that part of the Sea-Goat, and is currently at 13°41' **(Aquarius)**, 19°13' **Capricorn**. There is no special mythology attached to the star, apart from that of the Constellation, and so Ptolemy's identification of it as a Saturn-Jupiter type is the important thing about it. This is an important feature, since conjunctions of these two planets, which happen every twenty years, are invariably times of very important events in world affairs, usually with a stressful side to them but with an overall positive outcome. And individuals born with that conjunction prominent on their charts are well recognised as having a role in life, and the ability to play it, well beyond the average of their fellows.

The same planetry simile is given to the next three stars in **Capricorn**, ε, γ and δ, but not to β Aquarii which comes between them, and thus demolishes the charge sometimes thrown at Ptolemy: that he applied his similes in a meaningless 'blanket' manner. It does mean, however, that this whole last 10° of **Capricorn**, the second half of **(Aquarius)** also, is an important region concerned with the furtherance of human communal affairs, so that we shall do well to look at *Dorsum* and its three succeeding stars together.

Castra, ε Capricorni, is now at 20°2' **(Aquarius)** 25°34' **Capricorn**, and the name means a military camp or a Fortress. (The British towns with caster or chester in their names were once Roman fortresses.)

Nashira, γ Capricorni, at 21°36' **(Aquarius)**, 27°8' **Capricorn**, is from the Arabic *Al Sa'ad Al Nashirah*, The Bearer of Good News, and is one of those rare stars reckoned as 'good', even by the traditional astrologers. They saw it rightly as an indicator of social popularity and political success for the individual blessed with it on the chart.

Only 1°35' after that, we find β Aquarii, *Sa'adalsu'ud*, 'Luckiest of the Lucky', a Saturn-Mercury star (So who said Saturn is always a bad fellow?!) and then just 10' further on we have *Deneb Algiedi*, Tail of the Goat, a Saturn-Jupiter again. We are now at 23°20' **(Aquarius)**, 28°52' **Capricorn**.

The Arabs did not really separate these five stars for purposes of astrology: *Nashira* and *Sa'adalsu'ud* were the focal centre of a very good area of the sky which was all about good rulers and successful sheikhdoms, Saturn-Jupiter, and good things happening for their people, Saturn-Mercury. And they carried this benefic area on to include the stars *Sa'ad Al Malik*, Good or Lucky King, α Aquarii, and the mighty star of Archangel Gabriel, *Fomalhaut*, Mouth of the Fish, α Piscis Australis, with its reminiscence of that earlier star *Nunki (Pelagus)*, Edict from the Sea, or, freely interpreted, Word of God. These last two are now at 3° and 3½° **(Pisces)**, around 9° **Aquarius**.

All this must have meaning for those who are looking forward so keenly to 'The age of Aquarius', and it contains a message of hope that it may not be so far off as some have calculated. For the true constellational position of the Vernal Equinox, presently at 5°25' of **Pisces**, may not have to recede further than to 4°19' **Pisces** before meeting with the advancing Archangel with the Trumpet of Annunciation. Even so, this still amounts to seventy years away from now, so it will be wise not to spend out yet on 'special offer haloes' in advance. They may not be the required model when the time comes!

Seriously, though, this Saturn-Jupiter-Mercury area from *Dorsum* to *Fomalhaut*, concluding our survey of **Capricorn**, is an area of great hope for the world, and many of our greatest figures in humanity have its strength prominent in their horoscopes. A few examples are:

Tchaikovski, Verdi, Tennyson, Jules Verne, Clemenceau, Joseph Chamberlain, Eduard Benes; so two composers, two writers and three statesmen all among the most noted of their professions, all with their Midheavens on these stars, as had famed healer De Voe.

Toscanini, great conductor of Verdi, and humanist, is just one of dozens in the arts of all kinds with Venus here. Queen Victoria had Jupiter here, as did Marie Curie; Ronald Reagan and Charles Dickens have Sun here. Author-alchemist Rider Haggard had Moon here, as had Rosicrucian astrologer and healer Mme Max Heindel and Emperor Haile Selassie.

There are so many more that the list is bound to include some 'baddies' as well, but they all left their profound mark on history in a big way, which is what **Capricorn** is really all about.

CHAPTER 15

Aquarius the Water-Carrier

The Constellation and Sign of **Aquarius**, the eleventh member of our current Zodiac, is perhaps more shrouded in mystery than any other. Early students of astrology often find it difficult to remember that this is an *Air* Sign, along with Gemini and Libra, when they see it so obviously connected with water. Confusion as to the origins of this human being pouring water out upon the Earth goes back into very ancient times and cultures. In early Egypt, it represented the source of the Nile, the life-giving artery of that country, but with no good explanation of how a human came to be the pourer of that stream. The idea sometimes put forward today – that it shows Man irrigating the land with water taken from the river – is of course feasible, and this would account for the Air-Sign quality given to **Aquarius**, the other two such Signs depicting also the human species and a product of its mechanical inventiveness.

But that has a rather exoteric, mundane ring to it which, while not at all disqualifying that explanation, would certainly have had the later temple priesthood looking for some deeper, esoteric meaning.

And if we should expect to find a similar mundane theme attached to **Aquarius** in the civilisations around the river Euphrates, it quite certainly is not there. Far from regarding this as a Benefic Sign, it was associated with the Great Deluge, the water-vessel in it, 'Gu', being seen as overflowing rather than usefully pouring out its water, and, when a humanoid figure of some kind came to be included, it was not a man but a god, Ramman, 'god of the Storm'. The association of Aquarius with the satanic Saturn may also have begun in that way. We must remember that we are here dealing with the very ancient community around the City of Ur, by legend the first resettlement after the near destruction of all life on this planet, and thus predating Egypt. (The words *urn* and Uranus, both associated with this constellation, may well have their origins from Ur).

Earlier still in that area, however, **Aquarius** was portrayed without anyone visible to hold the urn, and it was known as Ku-Ur-Ku, Source of the Flowing (or Living) Waters, a clear association with not *a* god, but *God*. The association of *God* with Living Water needs no emphasis, of course, being found in the teachings of almost all the prophets of all religions. It is by the Grace of that water that life exists here at all – (we are ourselves 70% water) – and it is an interesting thought that Islam's second title for God, after Allah, is Al Rahman, the Gracious – (compassionate in some translations) – a word which may well derive linguistically from Ramman, even though the people of Ur made an evil force of it later on. (No wonder Abraham left them to it!) Needless to say, Islam does not include a human figure in portrayals of **Aquarius**, its name for which is 'Pourer of the Water'.

Aquarius, in summary then, set the scene in ancient time for the growth of life, humanity in particular, on a new plane or level – a level at which it is consciously aware of its Divine Source, the Living Water, as it rebuilds its communal life in the aftermath of its transformation, or mutation, by the Great Disaster. The Voice from the Ocean, symbolised by the star *Nunki* in **Sagittarius**, has directed Man to re-establish himself on land, the meaning of the Earth-Sign **Capricorn**; and now, in this eleventh Sign, is given understanding of his place in the Universe to such of his number who will read what is set before them.

'Verily in the heavens and the earth are Signs for those who believe. Likewise in your own creation, and in that of all the creatures that He spreads out in the earth are Signs for a people who possess firm faith.' (Al Quran, Sura 45, tr. by Muhammad Zafrullah Khan, Curzon Press edition.)

It is natural, then, that **Aquarius** is the Constellation and Sign of true astrologers and people who seek learning, not in that debased usage of 'Will I get the job? Will he drop his price for the car? etc.', but 'Where does humanity fit into the Greater Plan?' and 'How can we better understand our role from moment to moment, and work with It by our voluntary choice, not the present half-for, half-against workings of blind accident?'

Many, in and out of astrology, now predict that the next century, the 'Age of Aquarius', will see our old religions of dogma swept away but, unlike the damage they have suffered in this century from atheist revolutions, their place will be taken by a truly revolutionary, intelligent understanding of our role as His 'Regents upon the Earth'.

There are nine reasonably visible stars in **Aquarius**, though only three are commonly used by present astrologers. We shall mention the others but it will be seen that, in most cases, they are close in longitude to other stars of more prominence, which is why they are not much noted in their own rights.

The first of these is *Albali*, Al Sa'ad al Bula, the Lucky Swallower, ϵ Aquarii, effectively the first star in the Constellation. With its companions μ and ν, it lies above the α and β stars of **Capricorn**, seeming to 'swallow up' their light with its own brightness and so accounting for its name. Its current position is 10°45' **(Aquarius)**, 16°11' **Capricorn**, just 1°51' short of *Armus*. We can reckon its orb for astrological purposes to be 1°40', which overlaps the 1° of *Armus*, so that it can be taken to show a quality of helpfulness and extra energy to whatever *Armus* itself signifies on a particular chart.

Next is β Aquarii, *Sa'adalsu'ud*, 'Luckiest of the Lucky' to which we have already referred when discussing *Deneb Algiedi* in the previous chapter. Without repeating what we said there, this is one of the two most important **Aquarius** stars, included in every worthwhile astrological list. Just for the record here in its rightful chapter, the position is 23°11' **(Aquarius)**, 28°43' **Capricorn**. In the year 2092 it will be in **Aquarius** by Sign and Constellation together. We from our heavenly homes, and some among our children and grandchildren here in the flesh, should then be sure of some great flowering of good upon this planet, especially in social matters and inter-human relationships. Meanwhile, it is universally recognised as a Sign of Good Fortune for all who have it prominent on their horoscopes, though like all such promittors, it should not be abused. Gamblers especially should beware of taking foolhardy chances when planets in transit or progression on their horoscopes are aspecting it by squares, oppositions and the like.

Some astronomy books make mention of *Ancha*, Θ Aquarii, the name being Low Latin for the Hip or Haunch of the water-pourer, but it really is insignificant astrologically, lying as it does only a quarter of a degree short of the very important *Sa'ad Al Malik*, (*Sadalmelik* in many spellings), 'Luck, or Fortune, of the King'.

Sa'ad Al Malik, α Aquarii, but in fact now marginally less bright than β, is now at 3°6' **(Pisces)**, 8°38' **Aquarius**, another Saturn-Mercury type, like *Sa'ad AlSu'ud*, and with very similar meaning for us. Perhaps it is rightly now the less bright of the two, in these days when good fortune for kings is expected to be no more important, at best, than the same for everyone else. Yes, it is an indicator of the most brilliant success and favour for those in authority, and a sign that they will put it to good use if they have it well aspected.

But the Saturn-Mercury simile is surely a note of warning for any who would abuse good fortune or be miserly about sharing it, a warning reiterated by the proximity of the Archangel star *Fomalhaut* only 24' of arc later in longitude. People doing well in high places will do yet better to remember that they are being watched from places higher still, watchers who no doubt have an unbiassed interest in the well-being of everyone, king and commoner alike, in the case of the advance of the entire human species and the planet it dwells upon.

Sadachbia, γ Aquarii, at 6°20' **(Pisces)** 11°52' **Aquarius**, is yet another lesser-known star, astrologically, but this one really does deserve some attention. The name, in which the 'ach' is pronounced as if in German, not like 'atch' in English, is a poor rendering from the Arabic: Al Sa'ad al Ahbiyah, 'The Lucky One for Hidden Things, or for Tent-dwellers'. Ahbiyah is the plural of a word once common for a tent but also meaning any place of seclusion.

It is said that, when the Sun rises conjunct with this star, about February 25th, then all the worms and insects come out of their winter holes, and the tent-dwellers can move to their Spring pasture-lands. That is in the warmer climes of Arabia, of course, not London or New York. In about 1000 years from now the Vernal Equinox (0°**Aries)**) will conjunct *Sadachbia* at about 20° or 21° **Aquarius**. For the moment, the author leaves it to ingenious readers to predict what this will mean for insects and tent-dwellers!

For now, the meaning we find in this star is as an indicator of the right time for making moves, entering upon new ventures, and a likelihood of general success in enterprises if *Sadachbia* be well placed and aspected on the horoscope. Ptolemy did not record a planet simile for it but something like Venus-Mercury would fit quite well. He gave the same to *Deneb Adige*, Tail of the Swan, α Cygni, *(q.v)* which precedes it by 1°40' or so, and likewise has connotations of 'time to move on'.

Now we come to *Skat*, δ Aquarii, at 8°32' **(Pisces)**, 14°1' *Aquarius*, another Saturn-Jupiter star, by Ptolemy. Utter confusion surrounds the origin of the name, which looks like a Scandinavian rendering of Shat 'Sheep'. There is no Arab record of it that way, however. Another guess has been *Shak*, 'Shinbone', since that is its location on the water-pourer, but that should be spelt *Saq* anyway, so that is not to be favoured. Some Arab maps have been found to show it as *Al Shi'at*, 'The Wish', and that is probably the right answer.

That causes confusion with the major star *Scheat*, β Pegasi, at 29° **(Pisces)**, however, so that, having found the most likely meaning now for the name, we do best to keep it spelt *Skat*.

Obviously, the planetary simile gives it much the same nature and significance as the stars from *Dorsum* to *Deneb Algiedi* inclusive, but here we must see it as in the context of 'moving on', like the star before it. People with it strong for them are likely to be good leaders in any adventurous field of activity, physical, economic or social, and its name as 'The Wish' characterises well the astrologer's view of the eleventh Sign and House as the realm of hopes and desires. In that case, all should remember that wishes granted by fairies melt away with the next sunrise; those which endure do so because the beneficiary has worked to deserve them. Such is ever the combination of Saturn and Jupiter.

Just 6' longitude short of *Skat* is the un-named white binary star ζ Aquarii, right in the centre of the Urn from which the water is being poured. This star is of more interest to astronomers than to those who look for meaning but it does nonetheless draw attention to another significance in *Skat*, as the point from which Man's hopes and wishes may issue forth, provided, as we said, that he has earned them.

Another star which has found little notice from astrologers is λ Aquarii, chief star in the stream of water pouring from the Urn, and at present at 10°40' **(Pisces)**, 16°12' **Aquarius**. This is surprising if only because there is no other star of note closer than *Skat*, 2°8' short of it. Next after it is *Achernar*, α Eridani, 4°20' away. We have a choice of names, two of them Greek, one Hindi. *Gdor* (Γδωρ) means Water; *Ekhousis* (Σκχνσιs) means an Outpouring, and the Hindu name for a whole constellation with this as its chief star was the Hundred Physicians, *Catabhishaj*, who worked under the supervision of *Varuna*, goddess of the Waters.

Notwithstanding the author's dislike of having any gods but God, the name *Varuna* is the easiest of all those names to spell and pronounce in nearly any language (*waruna* in Arabic) so why should we not accept that all 'gods/goddesses' are but Signs of the myriad manifestations of The One, and opt for a nice easy name? *Varuna*, then, must mark for us a place in the horoscope where our ventures and plans are likely to get under way; also, from the connotation of Physicians, it should show up our capacities for Healing, as registered doctors or in the many complementary fields ('alternative medicine', if you like). No research has been done yet on this star but the author has made a quick check while typing this script and found five effective healers known to himself with items on or opposite it. (Remember that stars, being distant, are often effective opposite their position as well as upon it.)

We are left with one more Aquarian star, again an 'unknown' one, this being *Situla*, or *Al Satl*, or *Al Daluu*, all meaning a Jar or Bucket. A couple of Greek names, now in disuse, have the same meaning. The star, χ Aquarii, is currently at 16°30' **(Pisces)**, 21°56' **Aquarius**.

It cannot be counted a major star, scarcely visible with a Magnitude of 5.5, but it does continue the generally humanitarian themes we have been seeing throughout **Aquarius**, and it takes us on to connect with the Constellation of **Pegasus**, the α star of which, *Markab*, is just 1°17' past *Situla*.

And there we must leave *Aquarius*, one of the more difficult Constellations to deal with as a Sign, but richly rewarding for what a little effort with the intuition can show us of Man's noble part and place in this world and the Greater Scheme of which Earth is itself, like us, a valued and exciting part.

CHAPTER 16

Pisces the Fishes

Astronomically speaking, **Pisces** is, in the words of popular astronomer Patrick Moore, 'obscure and uninteresting'. And in his evergreen little *Observer's Book of Astronomy* (pub'd, Fred'k Warne Ltd/Inc), it has the distinction of having none of its stars given a mention by name. Its stars receive scarcely better attention from the astrologer either, only one being commonly mentioned, for none is brighter than Vis.Mag. 3.72, and even that one often drops to a figure of 4, not really visible without binoculars. We shall do just a little better than that, however, and at least mention four stars.

The Constellation as a whole is more interesting, however, for its significance throughout our history. In the sky it forms a shape like a huge tick, the apex just below the Ecliptic, the long arm ending just above it and at about 20° of Sign **(Pisces)**, the shorter arm rising farther up, almost perpendicular within the last two degrees of the Sign **(Aries)**. So almost the entire span of **(Aries)** is contained in **Pisces**, and the 'First Point of Aries', the Vernal Equinox is currently at 5°24'41" **Pisces**, which is why we call our present era the 'Piscean Age'.

Except in the totally different astrological system of China, and the barbarism of the Aztecs, this Constellation has been known as The Fishes in every culture, with only occasional local modifications to emphasise more the Waters in which the fishes dwell. Some early Arab references mention only one fish, Al Samakah, this being the line of stars in the long arm of the figure, while the short arm was the line or cord by which it was held (or caught), but it was also and more generally known as Al Samakatiin, or Al Hutiin, both meaning the Two Fishes. And that is how it is commonly depicted.

Stories about **Pisces** are many, the one I like best being that mentioned by Patrick Moore (Op.Cit.) Those eternal figures of love, Venus and Cupid, narrowly escaped from the giant Typhon by jumping into the river Euphrates. The goddess Minerva celebrated this drama by placing two fishes in the heavens, with a cord between them to tell that Venus and Cupid stayed together and lived happily ever after. No doubt they raised a fine family and all that, which underlines the significance of **(Pisces)** not only as the last Sign of the Zodiac, and the end of the story, but also as the Eternal Beginning, from which the First and all subsequent Signs have sprung, and thus All Creation with them.

And those two views of the Twelfth Sign are very characteristic of 'Piscean' people. Some seem to be of a nature patiently resigned to everything, having 'seen it all before', while others are optimistically looking forward to all that is new and about to come into being, be it the flowers of Spring or supersonic travel, or 3-D television, or the Messiah or the Mahdi. They are very much a people of broad but somewhat undefined interests, outside of a very discernible leaning to religion, but more inclined to be onlookers rather than activists like their neighbouring Aquarians and Arians. We must always be wary of judging people too quickly by their Sun-Signs, of course, remembering that the Sun just may be the only thing they have in it!

A last general comment which springs to mind from the Venus-Cupid story: the map of **Pisces** in the sky bears an uncanny resemblance to the layout on Earth of the *two* rivers, Euphrates and Tigris, their sources widely separated but their streams meeting at the head of the Persian Gulf. This configuration, in the region which we have now seen to be so much associated with the restoration of life and humanity on our planet, is itself of inescapable Piscean symbolism.

And now we turn our attention to the stars of **Pisces**.

We come first to β Piscium, *Fom Al Samakah*, and we may be surprised that this star has figured so little in astrology for, though faint like all others in **Pisces**, it does occupy a position well clear of any other commonly used star. It marks the Mouth of the Fish at the more southerly end of the string, and this is enough to cause confusion with the star *Fomalhut*, in the Mouth of the 'Southen Fish', the quite different Constellation, *Pisces Australis*. This may be why there has been reluctance to note and use it.

Happily, the Arab astronomer Al Akhsassi applied his intelligence and selected another Arabic word for Fish when naming β Piscium. So it is *Fom Al Samakah* (roll that into one word if you prefer). Akhsassi went a stage further and referred to it as being *west* of its partner in **Pisces**, rather than south, for it is indeed really south-west of it. So we can safely include it after all.

The current position of *Al Samakah*, to abbreviate it a little, is 18°41' **(Pisces)**, 24°7' **Aquarius**. (Appreciate that the arc of **Pisces** in the sky well exceeds the nominal 30° given to each Zodiac Sign). We have no help from Ptolemy on this one but the superlative work of the great, late astrologer and vizier Dane Rudhyar[1] comes to our rescue. In his revision of the psychic understanding of every degree of the sky by Elsie Wheeler and Marc Edmund Jones, Rudhyar reveals the

1 Dane Rudhyar: An Astrological Mandala; Vintage Books, N.Y. and Marc Edmund Jones: The Sabian Symbols in Astrology; Shambhala Pubs, Boulder.

nineteenth degree of **(Pisces)** thus: *'A MASTER INSTRUCTING HIS PUPIL: the transfer of power and knowledge which keeps the original spiritual and creative impulse of the cycle active and undeviated.'*

There is a kinship yet also a marked difference here from this star's near-namesake Fomalhut. Both have that connotation of great power and wisdom bestowed 'from above', yet, as we shall see when we come to it in Piscis Australis, Fomalhut and its Archangel Gabriel are very much to do with releasing us from the inertia of the past, and with opening up a new era for us. *Al Samakah*, by contrast, is about keeping us on course and in tip-top condition to see the present era through. If we were to give this a planetary simile, then, probably, Jupiter-Mercury is most appropriate: it has the right note of a message from the Divine Source to keep things running according to plan. And that, then, is the quality we should find in those with this star strong for them: They have that ability to be attuned to an inner sense of direction in fast-changing times, and to impart it to others.

There follows now a succession of stars along the string from β, including γ,Θ,ι,ω, δ,ε,μ, and γ, ending with α, and thus spanning the entire arc of the Constellation. Various of these have found favour with local regions of early astrology, Chinese, Indian, Sogdian, Persian, Coptic, Khorassian etc., but only as their particular markers for 'The Cord'. None before α is really of special import: it is really the total string which is characteristic of the cosmic nature of **Pisces** as a whole, a graspable link between ourselves holding the string at α, and the great 'Ocean' of the Universe from which the fish at β is being reeled in. Without the string, we should have no access to what lies still to be discovered and known, 'out there' and within ourselves. The prime star of the Constellation, α Piscium, is *Al Risha'*. The Cord (or String). This apparent double star, which may actually be a true binary pair, is at the point where the two arms of the figure meet. In some portrayals, the fishes themselves are at the far ends of the arms, so that the long string is folded at star α as though being held at that point.

In some Latin works this star is called The Node of the Fishes, or of the Two Strings, *Nodus Piscium* or *Nodus Duorum Filorum*, which describes the position precisely but has not remained in general usage. It is here mentioned only for the record, as also the Arabic rendering of the same title, *Al Ukd Al Haitain*, or *Ukda*, or *Kaitain*, with variations on those spellings. In general, the better name to use and remember is what we started with, *Al Risha*', though it is worth warning the reader that this name has also been used in the past for star β Andromedae, better known now as Mirach (q.v). However, *Al Risha*, is practically conjunct by longitude with the *Great Galaxy* in **Andromeda**; and this latter, a glorious family of billions of stars, must surely take precedence over the barely visible star α in **Pisces**.

If we take further note of *Al Risha* at all, it should be to think of it as the crux of a thread holding things together in the notoriously nebulous *Pisces*, and as a kind of lifeline to be thrown to those adrift in the Ocean of Time and Space. We shall see more of this when we discuss **Andromeda** separately; for now it is enough to say that people with this point strong in their horoscopes do have a better than average capacity for knowing where they are at, and where they are going, and a gift for helping others forward also.

Shortly before α in longitude we find η Piscium, *Kullat Nuni* or *Alpherg*, as it is commonly known by both names, and it is the only star of *Pisces* in common astrological usage. It lies in the shorter, northward running arm of the string and its present position is 26°38' **(Aries)**, 2°10' **Aries**, so that it has crept sidereally out of its old home since about 1846 A.D. In fact it crossed the point 0° **Aries** just at the time of the discovery of the planet Neptune, which was so soon to be recognised as co-ruler of **(Pisces)** along with Jupiter.

The origin of the Babylonian name *Kullat Nuni* is a little obscure now, but it was long thought to be, again, 'Cord of the Fish'. There is good reason, however, to interpret this as 'Home of the Fish'. This brings to mind the Sagittarian star *Nunki (Pelagus)*, the 'Voice from the Sea', symbolising the guidance which directed the early survivors after the Great

Disaster to make landfall and a new civilisation in the region later to become Babylon. So the 'Voice' and the 'Home' of the 'Fish', those who came from the sea, have much more in common than the mild similarity of the names *Nunki* and *Nuni*. It is further significant that the astrological Fishes themselves, both in and out of the Zodiac Signs, are known specifically by the stars in their mouths, *Fomalsamakah* and *Fomalhut*, in other words by their voices.

Kullat Nuni's later name, *Alpherg*, is of course Arabic, properly Al Fargh. The term means an outpouring of water, and the mouth or lip of any vessel used for water (or anything else). So there is the connotion of, again, something coming out of its container onto the earth and for the use of Man. Water inside a vessel is very much a hidden thing; we don't even know for sure that it is water until it is poured and tasted. Folklore abounds, of course, with tales of wine and water interchanging by magic within the flask, or emerging poisoned, or as the fire-creature the Jinn (or Genie) when Al Fargh is uncorked.

So this star of mysteries to be revealed to us, about ourselves, our distant origins, our Creator, was well classed by Ptolemy as another Saturn-Jupiter type. Those with it well placed in their horoscopes have ready access to, and understanding of, what the Church loves to call 'The Mysteries' (but is reluctant to reveal to us, if it knows them itself). Let those who have *Alpherg* poorly aspected beware of the Genie that may emerge if they uncork it by mere dabbling for occult kicks. Nothing that happens with a Saturn-Jupiter conjunction is on a small scale, neither enlightening revelation, nor pathological obsession with the past.

And there we leave the Constellations of the Zodiac, to venture elsewhere among the Living Stars.

CHAPTER 17

Beyond the Zodiac

One good popular book on astronomy lists 88 Constellations recognised today, of which only twelve form the ancient Zodiac. Of the other 76, quite a number were well known in early times, but many more were added by the enthusiastic astronomers of the 17th to 19th Centuries, especially as they explored the hitherto unnoted regions of the skies over our southern hemisphere. **Pavo**, the Peacock, for example, was introduced by Johann Bayer in 1603, as also was **Phoenix** along with several more from this German of fertile mind, while the Polish astronomer Johannes Helvelius added **Canes Venatici**, the Hunting Dogs, in the northern hemisphere, in 1690.

About 50 years later the Frenchman de Lacaille introduced **Fornax**, the Furnace, and **Circinus**, the Compasses (drawing instruments). We could list many more, including a Crane (bird) and a Pendulum Clock. As in traditional adoration of the heavens, living creatures predominate but the rise of European industrial growth was reflected in the number of mechanical devices, like the Compasses, the Furnace and the Clock, making for a huge percentage increase on the one man-made device in the Zodiac, **Libra**.

How is the intuitive reader of the Signs in the Heavens, priest or astrologer, to regard these new forms? Are they adulterations by an infidel group of materialists? Or truly new Signs which He, All Wise, has inspired those men to set before us for guidance in a new era? The present author shares entirely the view of the great Johannes Kepler, that there is nothing we do or discover that is not Divinely Ordained for our enlightenment if we will look for His Hand in it. Kepler himself, while working under the Danish astronomer, Tycho Brahe, had a hand in the introduction of *Coma Berenices*, Berenice's Hair, in 1602, though that is but a trivial item in the great mathematical work which he did on the motions of the planets.

In the present volume we shall not make much use of these newer Constellations, but the point is made here that they *should* be given our attention from now on, and the author for one will look forward to reading what others discover from them. We shall, however, be looking at thirty-one non-zodiac figures, one of which is a 'modern', two others being 18th Century subdivisions of an ancient Constellation.

We shall consider them in something like zodiacal order, though it will soon become clear that such a strictly formal approach will not suit our purposes if too rigidly followed.

One last point before we come to them. There are astrologers who hold that any star not on the Ecliptic should not be considered, and others who contend that a star is not to be taken into account if not in a part of the sky visible from the birth place of a personal horoscope. We leave them happy with a two-dimensional Universe bound to the Sun's path around Earth (or vice versa), and merely point out with a smile that the Sun itself was not visible to those attending upon someone born at midnight! Fortunately God gave us the means to know and record where stars are, even when our eyes cannot see them.

CHAPTER 18

Cetus the Whale

This huge creature, which extends just below the Ecliptic from about 1° (**Aries**) to the middle of (**Taurus**), has two major legends attached to it. On the one hand it is the Biblical Whale which swallowed Jonah and thus saved him to go on and become a prophet, while to the Greeks it was the Titan Sea Monster which came to devour Andromeda, and thus sometimes called *Balaena* instead of **Cetus**. Neither significance can be discounted by us, nor can its allegory for us as simply a whale, with all that creature's nature and behaviour patterns. We shall see this as we look four of its stars which matter most.

Our first star here is *Deneb Kaitos*, Tail of the Whale, β Ceti, but now actually brigher than α. It has the alternative name from an earlier Arab source: *Difda*, Frog, strictly the Second Frog, *Difda'l Thaniya*, the First Frog having been the star we now know as *Fomalhut*. In some cultures, frogs are said to be warners of what lies before us, probably because they inhabit bogs and croak at our approach. We have noted already that *Fomalhut (Difda'l Awwal)* is the star of that Divine Messenger Gabriel, generally announcing a good event to come, but a whale more often uses the slap of its huge tail upon the sea to sound a warning to its companions for several miles around it. Ptolemy gives this star the simile of Saturn, which fits the theme perfectly. The current position is 2°19' **(Aries)**, 7°51' **Pisces**, making it the first star in our present Zodiac, surely right for such an annunciator.

The problem with a whale slapping its tail to tell other whales something is that it sounds its presence to human whale-hunters too, to its great peril, even if we are *supposed* now to have stopped whaling. Making big waves without thought for the consequences is all too familiar an Arian problem, and people with this star less than well aspected on their charts really do bring trouble upon themselves very easily by speaking too much too soon. (Author first-class at this, having Moon there, square Ascendant). But if well aspected, we find people who are great at initiating new projects and ideas. This star fails to make much contact with **Andromeda** above it in the sky, so there is little of the evil Sea Monster about it.

Baten Kaitos, Belly of the Whale, ζ Ceti, at 21°40' **(Aries)**, 27°12' **Pisces,** is of course associated with the Jonah legend. Likewise a Saturn star by Ptolemy, it often does mark where someone becomes stuck with a situation for some little while, perhaps from their folly under *Deneb K*, but, aspects all being well, should emerge with some benefit to count for the experience, even honour from it if all is very well in the matter of aspects.

Stella mira, Wondrous Star, and *Collum ceti*, Neck of the Whale, are alternative titles for o Ceti, at 1°21' **(Taurus)**, 6°53' **Aries**. The first name comes from its extraordinary variability in brightness, from Vis.Mag. 1.7, by far the brightest in **Cetus** at certain times, to 9.5, needing a telescope to see it at all. The period of variation is about 330 days. Its proximity to β Andromedae does give us now a hint of the Sea Monster, with more than a hint that the monster was heading for trouble rather than a meal. A whale's neck contains its remarkable spouting organ, another feature which signals inadvertently its prescence to the hunters. Seen in another way, the whale looks very impressive, as does this star, even terrifying, but is in fact a gentle creature, and quite vulnerable in modern times. The Monster, too, is really all size, noise and puff when the chips are down as we shall see when we tell the story of **Andromeda**. Ptolemy did not classify this star, suggesting that it was less remarkable in his day, but Mars-Saturn, a gun with the safety-catch stuck, fits well. The well-aspected man will avoid fighting where Taurean peace will do him better service. Others may find they have rushed in needlessly and without a weapon any better than "sound and fury".

Last star in **Cetus** is *Menkar*, α Ceti, at 14°6' **(Taurus)**, 19°38' **Aries**. The Arabic name means Nostril; an alternative name is *Al Kaff* or *Al Qaf Al Jidhmah* both implying the nose area of this creature. It is yet another Saturn star, Ptolemy, and again it is one very close in longitude to an **Andromeda** star, α this time. Presumably it was the Monster's nose that led it to the young lady, with every expectation of a fine old Jupiter-Mars time(!) for star *South Scale* is right opposite *Menkar*. But as we said of that star, one has to consider intelligently the consequences of one's actions, and the Saturnine quality of *Menkar* is just right for this, if it be well aspected. It obviously was not so for the Titan, but it is a star which shows good practical sense in those better blessed with it.

Now we tell the **Andromeda** story, with all dramatis personae present.

CHAPTER 19

Andromeda and the Titan

Supporting Cast: *Cassiopeia; Cepheus; Medusa; Pegasus; Perseus;* An Owl.

King *Cepheus* and Queen *Cassiopeia* ruled Ethiopia, and she was much the more important of the two, a forerunner of the later Queen of Sheba. Like her, however, *Cassiopeia* was proud and haughty, and dared to boast that she was more beautiful than the Nereids, the sea-nymphs much loved by Neptune. He was greatly angered and demanded that the Queen's daughter, *Andromeda*, be chained to a rock in the sea, there to be eaten by the Titan sea monster whom Neptune commanded.

Perseus was a dashing young hero who, being handsome, caused some discord between Jupiter and his wife Juno. So *Perseus* was sent on the perilous mission to destroy the Gorgon *Medusa*, a female demon so terrible that even to look at her would turn the viewer to stone.

Jupiter gave *Perseus* a fair chance, however, and allowed

Minerva to lend the hero her shield. Even Jupiter himself provided a gold owl as a scout for *Perseus*, though he was alarmed when the bird led *Perseus* to find *Pegasus*, the last of Jupiter's herd of flying horses.

Using the shield as a mirror so that, without looking directly, he could see *Medusa's* reflection, *Perseus* cut off her head, put it safely in a bag, mounted *Pegasus* and was on his way back to Olympus when he looked down and saw *Andromeda*, with the Titan just approaching her.

The hero swooped down, pulled the head from the bag before the monster's eyes, turning it to stone at once. He wisely dropped the head into the sea without further ado, unchained *Andromeda*, married her and lived happily ever after. The princess did outlive her husband, however, and so is sometimes known as 'The Widow'.

This story has so many ramifications that we cannot give it full treatment here. The nub of it is that *Cassiopeia* was setting herself up for comparison with the gods and their kindred; and that act, whether in worship of, or in comparison to them, is one of looking backwards, of tying oneself to the past and to ossified falsehood in place of the living truth and the reality of *now*. Bilqis (Queen of Sheba) was to learn the same lesson more happily from Solomon later. The response of the primeval forces, worshipped by her as gods, within that ocean from which we sprang, the past, was to tie up and threaten to devour the Queen's future, symbolised by her child.

Perseus, as a name, can be understood as One who knows, or is, just himself as God had made him, not the slave nor adorer nor subject of any others. Only such as he can go into the past and destroy the forces that lurk there, yet even he may not look upon them directly lest he be caught up and ossified by them, as others are. That assertion can be challenged psychologically, it is true, but the experiences of psychoanalysis so far have shown it to be stronger than most of us would take a risk on, if we are wise.

Medusa, often associated with Lilith, is not really that ancestor of ours, but rather the tangled mash of traumas from the Great Disaster onwards, which now lie between us and the truth of our origins. It is because those who look back in search of Lilith must first encounter *Medusa's* ghoulish demons of fear and pain that Lilith herself has been confused with them. It is rather like the sailors who found America believing they had found India when only halfway there.

Pegasus, like birds, angels and most celestial winged creatures, is allegory for the superior spiritual power that the hero first sought out to aid him in his task, and the Owl represents the wisdom side of that same power. The story is now complete: Humanity has been rescued from the past and is freed again to go forward to its destiny in the Heavens. Note that *Andromeda* outlives her husband, symbolic of our need as mortals for the feminine, receptive quality to keep us attuned to that superior, Divine Source as we go on our upward way.

The *Stars* in this story must surely centre upon those of *Andromeda* herself and it is significant that α Andromedae, *Alpheratz*, is in both *her* Constellation and that of *Pegasus*. As we have just said, the lady is our link with the Divine Power. The name means The Horse, from days when it was associated with *Pegasus* alone, whereas now it is also the princess's hair. Appropriately for its role, it is a Jupiter-Venus type in Ptolemy's book, again the female-to-God link. And, well aspected, it does show strongly where our ability to attune to higher forces is very evident. Poorly aspected, it may show where we just pretend to Divine inspiration for less than worthy purposes. The current position is 14°3' **(Aries)**, 19°35' **Pisces**.

Before we reach that star, however, we must have encountered α and β Pegasi; respectively *Markab*, 23°13' **(Pisces)**, 28°45' **Aquarius;** and *Scheat* 28°59' **(Pisces)**, 4°31' **Pisces**. Both are Mars-Mercury types.

Both these stars are true-black malefics in traditional astrology, promising injury by one's hand or another's, and life imprisonment. We can now see how, in the times of profane use of astrology, this arose. At this far end of the

Zodiac, we find it easy to delude ourselves that 'now we know it all'; we can take our seats with the gods. '*Markab*' is commonly a ship, but may be used for any kind of conveyance, a saddle on a horse included, so off we go in or on it. If we did indeed learn what *Andromeda* had to teach us at the start of the journey, then fine, we can achieve 'Great Mastery', the occasionally mentioned positive signature of these two stars: all we could wish for, that being the meanin of *Scheat* (Al Shi'at). But if we started out rightly, then we should here have no need to exhibit that matery in secular power, nor should we still need to wish for more than we already have and are: 'My Kingdom is not of this world', as Jesus said so well. So we can easily recognise the quiet, unassuming, untroubled true master from the embattled, imprisoned, pathetic pretender to mastery.

All of that applies just as much to *Algenib*, γ Pegasi, at 8°54' **(Aries)**, 14°24' **Pisces**, another Mars-Mercury, its name, pronounced Al Zhaynib, meaning The Side (of the horse). Its placing in **(Aries)** since 754 years ago, now gives it extra impetus for better or worse, and shows something of that kind of Master who feels perhaps that the old-style secrecy in which his fellows used to surround themselves should now give place to a more open attitude, at least to such of the laity as show a willingness to listen and learn.

After that in longitude comes *Alpheratz*, already discussed, then the famous *Great Galaxy in Andromeda*, Messier M31, and earlier called the Great Nebula. It is interesting to read in a book as recent as 1899: 'Its true (astronomical – E.M.) character seems as yet undetermined, although astro-photography has proved it to be a vast saturniform body. . .'. Only in our century was it recognised as a galaxy much like our own, saturniform because galaxies seen nearly edge-on, with bulbous centre and thin disc, do look like Saturn and its rings.

Its present position is 27°38' **(Aries)**, 3°15' **Aries**, and Ptolemy classed it malefically as a Mars-Moon type, about as bad as can be! Someone has unfortunately given it the name *Vertex*, which is used for a quite different kind of item in astrology, so it is better to call it *Great Galaxy* or *Andromeda Galaxy*. It really is one of the most potent Signs in this part of the sky, revealing to us, if well aspected, the person who has great gifts for treating sicknesses of neurosis, psychosis or obsession; otherwise it shows up just the people suffering most from those very Mars-Moon problems deep within them from the past, personal or collective.

Mirach, β Andromedae, at 0°13' **(Taurus)**, 5°45' **Aries**, takes us past the lady's most critical stars so that, reasonably, Ptolemy gives this a pure Venus rating. The origin of the Arabic name is obscure, so that earlier western commentators muddled it with Mizar, a girdle, roughly its position on the figure as now commonly drawn. The closely similar name 'Merak' (β Ursa Major) means the loins or genitals, and yet another very similar word means 'womanly'. Still another means 'to let milk flow'. It all depends on where we see it on the anatomy of this lady, who has been redrawn since she gained a star from Pegasus. An etymological connection with either or both the Virgin Mary and the Archangel Gabriel (in Arabic) is not impossible. All of these which emphasise the feminine and the Divine qualities are more in keeping with the *Andromeda* we know, better fitted to Ptolemy's Venus simile.

The careful, well attuned gentle approach, then, is what we should find from people with this star well aspected; otherwise there may be an over-timid attitude, perhaps markedly effeminate in a male.

Our next star in the story is α Cassiopeiae, *Schedir* in most modern spellings, a mishandling of the emphatic Arabic S in Al Sadr, the Breast. It lies at the more acute apex of the large W in the sky which represents the Queen on her throne. Position now is 7°43' **(Taurus)**, 13°15'**Aries**. There is no Ptolemaic classification for any of her stars, surprising for such a clearly visible figure, but this may be because of *Schedir's* near-conjunction with *Hamal* of **(Aries)**. The queen's capacity for disastrous bombast suggests the same Mars-Saturn simile we find with *Hamal*, save for the generous gratitude she showed then to *Perseus*, so Mars-Jupiter seems the best likeness. The man or woman with this star strong may have great qualities to rule over others, but should beware of letting it go to his/her head.

We come now, chained anatomically, to the end of **Andromeda**, the Foot by which she is chained, *Almach*, or *Alamak*, γ Andromedae, at 14°8' **(Taurus)**, 19°40' **Aries**. By some accounts, this is a burrowing animal, having nothing to do with the Constellation we know, but the present author has found fairly similar words meaning 'deep in water', as her foot must have been, then 'a clasp', holding her there, and another word meaning 'exemplary punishment', which also fits this story. Ptolemy makes a pure Venus of this star, a very touching tribute to *Andromeda's* patience during her ordeal. When well aspected it does reveal great patience, the best of Taurean qualities, though it is so close (0°3) after *Menkar*, α Ceti, that we must take account of what we have said of that star also. We may add that the patience shown here may well spring from a firm faith and trust in Divine help, as the lady must have needed with the monster's nose that close to her!

The stars of the Hero are the last ones to appear in the story. We first have *Capulus*, or *Gyrus*, a multiple star and a cluster, close together at 24°16' **(Taurus)**, 29°48' **Aries**, known to astronomers as M34, 33hVI Persei, or NGC 884 & 869.

The second name merely describes their circular appearance but *Capulus* means a Handle, as they mark the sword-hand of *Perseus*, which is why Ptolemy classed them as a Mars-Mercury item. Like most clusters they are traditionally malefic, associated with either murder or execution. Being in Taurus, those fates are specifically related to the neck, hanging or beheading.

The same applies to the next star, *Algol*, alias *Caput Medusa*, the Demon herself, but much more so. Indeed she is without doubt counted the most malefic of all stars in astrology, even though Ptolemy gives her the less obviously ominous Saturn-Jupiter styling. Medusa's Head, the meaning of the Latin title, is being held in *Perseus's* hand, which is why she is star β in his Constellation, at 26°8' **(Taurus)**, 1°40' **Taurus.**

What seems to have been missed by the old school is that *Capulus* and *Algol* (now the more usual names) each have a very positive side to them. That sword did remove a monstrosity from our world, and the monstrosity's head did, in its turn, rescue *Andromeda* – and by the same token, all of us – from yet another monster of great evil. True that *Algol* comes from an old Arabic word meaning particularly nasty spirit but then, as we have noted, we all too easily look back and within ourselves only to be halted at our traumas and 'nasty bits', failing to penetrate further to the glory beyond them. Lilith is not Medusa at all, not the ugly blockage in us but the beauty beyond it. Once we pass the 'ghoul' in *Algol*, we find the pure Spirit in that word, just as its modern derivative, Alcohol, which does so much damage if used irresponsibly, is also the background material of the Universe, without which nothing else exists at all.

How *Capulus*, and more especially *Algol*, signify on horoscopes depends entirely on how the person concerned does or does not live life with an honest sense of purpose to it, a desire at least to *try* to live up to some kind of philosophy, religion or ideal. If that be present, in the person or question or event for which the chart is drawn, then all will go well. The author has seen this happen so often, once the superstition about these stars is dropped. If purpose and intent be 'shady', then we don't really need stars to tell us that things are likely, with good reason, to go wrong.

Yes, we know that *Algol* often does show up in disastrous accidents with death as their climax, but we must remember then our too-common state of disbelief in life beyond the one event since birth that is the lot of us all. We fear because we do not believe, and we fear to overcome our fear, lest to be fearless of death should somehow cause us to love mortal life the less. We fear to let go of the past because we lack faith in the Hand that holds the future. With *Algol* poorly aspected in our charts we may well repeat the popular but obscene: 'Better the devil you know than the devil you don't', but those with the Star of the Spirit better placed, we find the person who knows better than to slander that Hand as a devil. Many a fine counsellor and healer has *Algol* thus placed.

CHAPTER 20

Orion the Hunter

Approximately a large X in the skies beneath **Taurus** and **Gemini**, **Orion** is one of the most popular and easily seen constellations. Even non-astronomers can usually recognise at least 'The Belt' of three stars at his waist. The name as we have it now is actually a short form of the earlier 'Warion', Ωαριων, whence comes our word warrior.

He seems to have been a real personage at some time long past, and was then called Kanda'on, Κανδαων, a name related to Alexander, which itself means a helper of others.

But in mythology he was a demi-god, son of Neptune and Euryale, and unfortunately shared Cassiopeia's talent for boasting. He claimed he could fight and slay any animal of any size, and took on *Taurus* the Bull to prove it. Juno was jealous of him, she preferrring her female warrior Diana, and so she sent little *Scorpio* to sting him in the foot just as the Bull was about to meet its 'moment of truth'. Jupiter, not liking his wife's display of female chauvinism here, because he was a male chauvinist himself(!), placed *Orion* honourably in the sky, but opposite to Scorpio so that the hunter should not be troubled again. Now the warrior fights on harmlessly against the Bull, but with little Lepus the Hare under his feet as an alternative target, and with two Dogs, *Canis Major* and *Minor* to assist in that pursuit. But we shall treat those separately.

To make use of all **Orion**'s stars would be overdoing things, like the warrior himself, so we restrain ourselves to six of them.

The first is β Orionis, *Rigel* (pronounced Rizhel) and meaning the Foot. It is his forward foot, nearest to the bull. It is a very bright star, Vis. Mag. 0.08, and even brighter by true luminosity, being some 50,000 times more powerful than our Sun. The present position is 16°32' **(Gemini)**, 22°4' **Taurus**. Classed by Ptolemy as Jupiter-Mars, it invariably shows a character that will take on anything before it, but such a person does have to be careful that their courage is used with wisdom and sincere purpose if they are not to be painfully stung for flaunting bravado for the sake of vanity.

Bellatrix, γ Orionis, is the Mars-Mercury star on his forward, left, shoulder, from which his arm reaches out to carry his shield. The name means the Female Warrior, or the Amazon Star, calling to mind the association with Diana, Orion's lady counterpart and sometimes said to have been his wife. One perhaps suspects Juno's influence here, for the real Amazons were a female-ruled community around Greece who fought ferociously against the wild hordes invading from Asia and bringing male domination with them. Again it is a star revealing great courage, but a tendency to fight futile or lost causes if it is not well aspected. To the Arabs it was Al Najid, the Conqueror.

The Belt comprises three stars, *Alnitak, Alnilam* and *Mintaka* in order from Orion's back to his front. They are respectively ζ, ε and δ in the Constellation. The first name means simply Belt, the next the Pearls (studs in the belt), the third is another word for Belt.

Alnitak is effectively conjunct with *Ensis*, the sword so we do not include it any further.

Mintaka, however, does receive the award from Ptolemy of a Saturn-Mercury styling, even though it is hardly separable by longitude from *El Nath* in Taurus. They are about 30° apart in declination, once used more in astrology than now. The position is 22°8' **(Gemini)**, 27°40' **Taurus**. This proximity to the bull's Horn inspires us to see Orion's belt stars as protection for him, and so this star does show that quality in our horoscopes if well aspected: we protect others and are ourselves protected. To that extent, it moderates the Mars effect of *el Nath*, but at the same time warns not to take silly risks for the sake of 'bullfighting' our way in life.

Alnilam has a generally brighter message with its pearls or jewels on the belt, and its Jupiter-Saturn simile. It is the signal of being able to do really great things if it is well aspected, and to be well rewarded as a result. Otherwise, however, it can reflect much of the useless bravado and show of some (not all) whom we see around at present with glittering studs all over their leather jackets, and nothing better to fight about than whether the rival gang has long or short hair! It is now at 23°14' **(Gemini)**, 28°46' **Taurus**.

Our next is ι Orionis *Ensis*, Latin for Sword, the scabbard of which hangs from the Belt. The Arabic alternative name *Hatysa* is obscure but may come from Hilya(t), Jewellery, or from Mahtassr, the Point of Death. In some drawings, Orion is holding his sword in his hand so that its point is just about on this star. Having a Mars-Moon rating, it is not generally accounted a 'good star' but, as always, that depends on the user of a gift for putting aggressive energies to practical effect. If the effect be a worthy one, then fine; but if not, then not fine. Position: 22°48' **(Gemini)**, 28°20' **Taurus**.

Betelgeuze, α Orionis, completes our picture, and a mighty star it is by any reckoning, for it is a red giant that would swallow Earth and Mars if it were to take the place of our Sun. It is at 28°33' **(Gemini)**, 4°5' **Gemini**. The name springs loosely from 'Armpit of the Giant' in Arabic, for it marks his right shoulder, but it can just as well mean Bayt Al Jauz, Home or Resource of the Giant, being on the main muscle that wields his sword. It is of Mars-Mercury classification, and never fails to reveal immense strength in a horoscope. Again, how that serves or fates the person in question depends on how he uses his strength. Nothing happens by halves if this great star is the Sign of it. We can only add 'woe to the radio-TV comic who renamed it Beetlejuice'! Yet may his popularisation of one of Heaven's great wonders plead for him.

It is a pity to leave out the other corner of **Orion**, the trailing foot, *Saif* (or *Saiph*). The name is the common Arabic word for Sword, so we must imagine the tip of the scabbard reaching down to **Orion's** rear foot as he is lunging forward. We do not have a planetary simile for it from the usual source, but a Mars-Saturn note of strength in reserve fits well. The Position now is 26°29' **(Gemini)**, 1°57' **Gemini.**

CHAPTER 21

Eridanus the River

In Xanadu did Kubla Khan
A stately pleasure-dome decree:
Where Alph, the sacred river, ran
Through caverns measureless to man
Down to a sunless sea.
S.T. Coleridge

Name almost any river greater than a village stream, and it has been sacred to some community at some time. And if the river be purely allegorical, like that in the poem above, then it flows through places where man cannot go and ends in a darkness we cannot penetrate. Water, the means of life, springs up from the depths to flow past as we catch what we need of it, and then is lost to our reach in the salty ocean. Its rivers symbolise all the mystery of where life comes from, what it is for, and for how long, and where it is leading us.

Scholars have long debated which particular earthly river

Eridanus may be, but it is all and none of them, just like the Styx or Kubla Khan's Alph, the first letter of Creation. From its Latin root, Eridanus is that which comes from the Master, raises us to life, then takes life from us as, in the words of a famous hymn: 'Time, like an ever rolling stream, bears all its sons away.' And in Edwin Arnold's 'Light of Asia' the cyclic nature of life is exemplified by the river which gives its water to the sea, only to receive it back again as rain as the Sun evaporates the sea to form new clouds.

Of this long Constellation, sixth largest in the sky, just four stars concern us here. First is *Achernar*, α Eridani, at 14°59' **(Pisces)**, 20°31' **Aquarius**. The name means End of the River, for it lies almost 58° south of the Equator beyond the sight of either Arab or Greek astronomers. Only since the 18th Century has it been included in the River, of which it is now chief star. Books list it as having a Jupiter styling from Ptolemy, and there is no reason to deny such a fine star that honour, but Ptolemy did not even know if it!

The star that he knew by that name and Jupiter styling was θ Eridani, now renamed *Acamar*, at 8°9' **(Taurus)**, 13°36' **Aries** and at a declination of only 40° south, where the River once ended. Both stars, however, carry in astrology a note of one who is blessed with a direct line, as it were, to the Source of All Being, and who is able to bring back something to fortify his or her position in this world. *Achernar* almost never fails to show this up in the horoscope, unless severely afflicted by aspect, when it may indicate a show of 'all's well' more than the real truth of the situation.

Acamar needs better aspect to make the same grade, and its proximity to α Cassiopeia, *Schedir*, increases the possibility of a pretender to honour and fame, rather than one who really has them. Even so, it is very far from being a 'malefic', and both stars often do reveal a high degree of spiritual attunement on the horoscope.

Zaurak, γ Eridani, is at 23°22' **(Taurus)**, 28°54' **Aries**, and the name comes from Al Na'ir al Zaurak, the Bright one on the Boat. Ptolemy seems not to have bothered with it but

Joseph Rigor (who mis-spells it Zanrak) gives it a bad name for melancholia and feelings of great loneliness, as though one is all alone on that long river. It is indeed close to the markedly difficult *Capulus* (M34 Persei), and it is only a short way down the river from the start of the journey. So, yes, there can be that feel of 'it's a long way to go'. Yet, if the aspects be right, there can also be that forward-looking faith that one is not really alone, that He truly is there at *Achernar*, and even Rigor has had to note that this star features with many fine writers and poets of great inspiration. So if Ptolemy had classified it, he would probably have made it a Saturn-Mercury.

Finally we have *Cursa*, β Eridani, most northerly star in the river and effectively its source spring. It is at 15°18' **(Gemini)**, 20°45' **Taurus**, and only 3° from Orion's foot, *Rigel*. The name in fact comes from the Arabic for 'The giant's Footstool'. Although bright, Vis. Mag. 2.9, it is far outshone by *Rigel*, and this can be read as the inspiration to set out upon the long quest to the Divine Source of that brightness. The weariness to come, marked by *Zaurak*, lies far away yet, so *Cursa* is a Sign of Enthusisam for the Quest, surely meriting a Jupiter-Mercury simile. Look for that enthusiasm in those that have this star strong and well aspected.

CHAPTER 22

Boötes the Herdsman

Around our North Pole is a varied collection of animals, dominated by the two Bears, Great and Little. Descriptions of this 'mini-zodiac', which does indeed extend all the way round the sky, have varied much from one age to another, the bears apart, and have included cattle as well as creatures of the wild.

Naturally there has to be someone there to maintain order and to protect those in the service of God and man, and that is precisely the role of the Herdsman, *Boötes*, the subject of our cover illustration.

His name has long been something of a puzzle, for there are several possible sources for it in the Greek. The probability is that the name comes from a word meaning to shout and clamour, for well armed though he is, he is a protector of all creatures, and does not strike with his weapons if fearsome noise will assert his authority instead. This is certainly how the Arabs interpreted the name, for they made him Al Awwah, the Barker, and also gave him charge of a dog, which the Hebrews before them had managed to see there with him. The name Al Awwah has another significance too, being close to Al Awwal, 'the First' implying closeness to God, if not even God Himself. That was in pre-Islamic times, of course; no such human representation is countenanced now. But The Quran does speak of man as a Regent placed upon Earth, with dominion over other creatures, so Al Awwal can be read that way too. Boötes then represents not God but all of us, in the role that God has given us to fill.

Prime star of Boötes is *Arcturus*, at one time the name for the Constellation itself, meaning the Driver of the Bear, Arctos (which is why our northern polar region is called the Arctic, of course). The Great Bear is obviously the most formidable creature there, and the point of Boötes' spear is menacingly close to the bear's rump in case shouting alone should not be enough.

Arcturus is a fine big yellow star, easily seen if one follows down a little from the curved sweep of the Bear's stars (the handle of The Plough, or Dipper), and one may continue the sweep down to the horizon to meet the all-important *Spica*, Ishtar, Queen of Heaven. The two stars are almost conjunct by longitude, leading the Arabs to see Arcturus as her protector: Al Haris al Sama, Protector of Heaven, and Al Haris al Samak, Protector of the Defenceless One.

So there we see the role of *Arcturus:* a protector, yes, but an unbiased protector of all. While we take what we may from *Spica*, from this symbol of the Heavens and Earth together, we are protected. But abuse that bounty, or take it from others, or deny it to them, and the Regent-Protector steps in upon us as upon any other predator. We are ourselves that same Regent, of course, so that it is our own hand and deed that calls us sharply to order. That is why older texts warn of *Arcturus* above the inviting *Spica*, as though God has maliciously placed a 'bad' star right on a 'good' one. One must marvel at the debased kind of astrology that does not accept a need to give as well as to receive of life's bounties.

Classed perfectly by Ptolemy as a Mars-Jupiter star,

Arcturus is now at 23°56' **(Libra)** 29°28' **Virgo**. It is, of course α Boötis.

In the herdsman's head we find β Boötis, *Nekkar*, a faulty transliteration of *Al Baqqar*, The Hersdman. Fine star though it is, it adds nothing but a slight extension to the orb of *Arcturus*, for its is only 45' past it in longitude.

On his left shoulder Boötes has star γ *Seginus*, a word coming from the Latin for a corn-crop, and thus meaning a reaper or harvester. In some illustrations he holds a reaping sickle in this hand. To the Arabs it is *Al Haris*, the Guard or Protector. It is at 17°14' **(Libra)**, 22°46' **Virgo**, and with its Mercury–Saturn simile it emphasises the protective nature of *Boötes*, and ourselves. The planetary connotation also shows up well the potential for writing and speaking in those who have it on their horoscopes.

The same connotations and planetry simile exactly are found with *Princeps*, δ Boötis, on the point of the Herdsman's spear. The name means Prince in latin, but many astronomers do not name it at all. It is also called Tsieh Kung, one of the very few retentions from early Chinese astrology, and meaning the Seven Princes, so the Latin title is really a recent rendering of that theme, and in some minds connects the star with the very nearby *Coronoa Borealis* more than with **Boötes**. There is no reason to disallow this, the reasoning that reads the Signs in the Heavens not being the narrow 'adding machine' of the left side of our brain. So again here, at 2°22' **(Scorpio)**, 8°16' **Libra**, we have another marker of our capacity to protect and be protected, but with a good hint of our role as Regent princes, and of the Crown that is ours for doing the job well.

Of very deep meaning to us is the star *Izar*, ε Boötis, at 28°20' **(Libra)** 4°39' **Libra**. From long before present constellational system was recognised, Epsilon Boötes was revered by ancient peoples, especially in Africa and South America, as the star from which their ancestors had first come to this planet. Since it is 150 light years away, the story is unlikely to say the least. But it is quite uncanny that this binary star's components are in relationship to each other almost exactly as Sun and Phaethon must have been before the Great Disaster began.

It is reasonable to suggest, then, that early astronomers discovered the kinship of the *Izar* binary to our own former state, and that their findings were announced by the media of the time, not as 'This is like what we came from', but 'This is where we came from'. We can imagine the popular press doing the same now.

The notion certainly took very deep root in us for, while the name Izar is merely Arabic for a girdle, its position on the figure, the word is frequently associated with Czar, Shah and other such terms for a father-figure to the community.

Early western students of astrology confused the name Izar, which can also be spelt Mizar, with Mirach, the name of β Andromedae, but this is in itself that kind of 'inspired mistake' which points again to the theme of *Izar* as a source of life to us, and a point from which to look forward, as we saw with β Andromedae itself. The result is that those with *Izar* strong for them do have both the keen interest in our origins, and a protective nature that wants to see us go safely on into our future development as a life species. Ptolemy did not apply himself to *Izar*, so far as we know, but a Saturn-Venus quality would seem entirely appropriate.

CHAPTER 23

The Two Bears

One popular astronomer friend of the author managed to find a third bear in the sky, at some cost to Boötes, and thus prove Divine authority for the much loved childrens' story. Andromeda still faced being eaten up, but now as Goldilocks, and by bears instead of a Titan. We, however, must stay with older tradition, tempting though it is to brighten our burden of archetypes with a little levity.

Ursa Major and **Ursa Minor** are among the oldest and best known of our celestial zoo, the smaller containing our Pole Star, the larger pointing it out clearly to us. No other two figures above us are in such constant practical use by people in almost all walks of life. The most easily discernible part of **Ursa Major** has long been treated as a different figure altogether: **The Plough**, or as the **Big Dipper** (Ladle or Pan) to Americans, whose westward pioneers had nothing else to guide them across their continent. They have now honoured it with place upon the state flag of Alaska.

All the stars which we consider here are from the **Plough,**

Dipper, along with the Pole Star and one other from the Little Bear.

Polaris, α Ursa Minoris, the Pole Star, is in fact our first star. Not as bright as we might wish, it is still easy to find by following up a line through the lower and upper stars at the end of the pan part of the **Dipper**. Its present position is 28°22' **(Gemini)**, 3°54' **Gemini**. Ptolemy gives it Saturn-Venus rating, entirely right for the star which serves so well to guide us in our wanderings. and that is just what it tells us about people when we find it strong on their horoscopes. According to its aspects, they are excellent or not so good at receiving and giving guidance, but give it they always will, and to any and all who will listen.

Kochab, β U-Minoris, takes its name from the Arabic *Al Kaukab*, simply 'The Star', for beyond 1000 years ago it was more nearly our Pole Star than the one we use now. And the same name was used, only a little differently spelt, in Babylonian and other pre-Arabic tongues. The Earth's tilt has been changing gradually ever since the Disaster, so our present Pole Star has only acquired its status (and name) by succession from a long lineage of polar indicators. *Kochab* is now at 12°37' **(Leo)**, 18°9' **Cancer**, close in longitude to α Cancri, *Acubens*. It is noteworthy that the latter star has just the Saturn-Mercury simile that goes with a guiding quality, like the Saturn-Venus of *Polaris*, so that, in the absence of attention from Ptolemy, *Kochab* can be given either of those ratings. Being in the **(Leo)–Cancer** region, it will often show in people a more reliable capacity for guiding than does the less mature, Geminian, *Polaris*.

Just on past *Acubens*, we come to the first of our **Ursa Major** stars, the α of the Constellation, *Dubhe*, or *Dubb* the Arabic for Bear. It is on the creature's back and, on the **Dipper**, it is at the lip of the pan end, pointing the way to *Polaris*. The position is 14°52' **(Leo)** 20°24' **Cancer**. We get no help from Ptolemy here, but the function of *Dubb* in pointing us to our chief guiding star tells us that those gifted with it, while they may not have all the expertise themselves, will certainly know where to send others for help, and will delight in doing so. A Mercury-Venus simile is not far amiss.

Merak comes next, the star beneath *Dubb*, helping it to point the way to the Pole for us. *Merak* is β U-Majoris, and the name comes from *Al Maraqq*, the loin (of the Bear). We need take little note of that; its role is the same as that of *Dubb* in every respect, and this will to play a guiding part, yet not quite in the leading place, is typical of this region of **(Leo)**, not quite equal to mighty *Regulus*. The position of *Merak* is 19°19' **(Leo)**, 24°51' **Cancer**, and again it has a Saturn-Mercury nature, perhaps with a little of the Mars drive that we find with ϵ Leonis just after it.

We are at 0°8' **(Virgo)**, 5°39 **Leo** for the next **Ursa Major** star, γ *Al Phecda*. The name is, again, anatomical: the Thigh of the Bear. In the **Dipper** it is at the bottom of the pan, below the handle-joint. Only 32' past *Regulus*, it should not be seen as a major symbol in itself, but rather as a reminder to those in power that strength, as in Bear, is only a part of their majesty; provision for others, as in Big Dipper, is what they are holding in trust. And if that Dipper does happen to be panning for gold, so well and good, but that too is to be shared if any of it is to be safely kept by the finder. A Jupiter-Venus simile seems needed here, to modify the Mars-Jupiter of the Star of Kings.

Magrez, the δ star of the Great Bear, is rather fainter than its neighbours, and joints the pan of the **Dipper** to the Handle. Its name means 'Root of the Tail', for the Handle is also the Bear's tail. Being effectively conjunct with *Al Phecda*, we need not take separate account of it.

Alioth, ϵ U-Majoris, is at 8°39' **(Virgo)**, 124°11' **Leo**, first star along the Dipper's handle from the pan. The Arabic name, Al Alyat, means the fat tail or rump of a sheep (or man, if rump), but has here been applied to the thickest part of the Bear's tail. (No living bear, of course, actually has a long tail like this celestial pair). Again, it has the same guiding significance as for the last few stars, but we need not count it as especially important, beyond that nature of help and service to one's fellows so characteristic of **Virgo** generally.

Next along the tail is star ζ *Mizar*, which, as we now know from other stars we have looked at, means a girdle or waist-band. There is no traceable reason for this name appearing here, and it is almost certainly an early western mis-spelling of *Mirza*, Prince, for the next star along likewise signifies a man of authority. In both cases, of course, the titles come from a culture which saw other than a bear in these stars, or did not allow the Bear this long tail.

We have to keep to the wrong name, which is now too well established, but we should allow that *Mizar/Mirza* does show more than average authority in the Virgoan role of service to one's fellows, sharing in that tendency to power which shows in all stars in the mid-point of a Sign. This one is in fact at 15°24' **(Virgo)**, 20°56' **Leo**. The same Saturn-Venus nature found with its zodiacal neighbours *Zosma* and *Denebola* fits it perfectly.

That next star which we spoke of is *Al Kaid*, or Al Qa'iid, coming from a variety of words meaning a tribal chief, an appointed local governor and the like. Often written *Alkaid*, it is η U-Majoris, at the tip of the tail, 26°37' **(Virgo)**, 2°9' **Virgo**.

Again, here is that greater note of authority, with responsibility for others, perhaps at a more immediately practical level than in the case of the Prince. The full title of this star, Al Kaid al Banaat al Na'ash, however, means Lord of the Daughters of the Bier, a funeral theme suggestive of the Weeping Sisters, *Alcyone*, to which this star is locked in trine aspect. So, then, the service required of the person with it strong on the horoscope may well be in the field of consoling people in the distress of bereavement.

If we are to give it a planetary simile, therefore, something like Moon-Mercury is on the right lines. But *Al Kaid* is so close in longitude to *Zavijava (Al Araph)* as to only give a little extra force to the meaning and the Mercury-Mars qualities we saw there.

CHAPTER 24

Man's Best Friends

Only the horse rivals the dog for the appellation which is our chapter title here, and the dog is often said to have actually *volunteered* to ally itself with Man in the distant primitive past.

There are four dogs, in three Constellations, in our skies: **Canis Major, Canis Minor,** and **Canes Venatici**.

The first of these, **Canis Major**, the Great Dog, is a tiny group dominated by the star *Sirius*, inevitably α by Greek letter, at 13°54' **(Cancer)**, 19°39' **Gemini**, coming along behind **Orion** the Hunter.

It is one of the most magnificent sights in our night sky, so near, only 8.7 light years away, and so bright with its Vis. Mag. 0.06, that it shimmers even to the naked eye. With just modest binoculars to help, it is a glorious blaze of auroric colour that leaves us wondering if it is really justice to classify it as 'white'.

The name comes to us from the Greek σεριος, 'scorching'

or 'fiery'. In Arabic it is *Al Suhail*, the Gleaming One, and in all other cultures its title has been along the same lines. It is held also to have been one of the very few stars on view to our ancestors even when we had only two brief twilights daily between our two suns in the sky.

It has been said also that this star takes its name from the Egyptian god-figure *Osiris*, but the truth is probably the other way round. The great leader and teacher of the Egyptians in the time of recovery from the Disaster has in all likelihood been remembered by the name of the brightest star in the heavens.

The present position, only one degree from the centre of **(Cancer)**, the place of Exaltation of Jupiter, and so-called 'Centre of the Universe', is shared with another very bright star *Canopus*, but of course we cannot say that either of them has always held this position. Nonetheless, *Sirius* has always been accorded that kind of status, which is why Ptolemy gave it a Jupiter-Mars simile.

So many wondrous tales are told around it that we just cannot repeat them here, but it has often been given a Divine significance even above the four Archangel stars. Its connection with a Dog comes without doubt from the early Hindu title for it. *Sivaanam*, the Dog which in the Rig Veda awakens the gods of the air and calls them to send the rains to restore life to the Earth. The later association with helping Orion to hunt a mere hare, or even to fight a bull, is just too pathetic to be taken seriously for a star such as this.

On horoscopes, *Sirius* marks immense creative talents in any field at all with 'only' the warning that here may be more inner power than can be safely managed. Harshly aspected it can show a psychotic person truly a menace to himself and the community, but in better condition we have here the star of the truly Great figures in every field of human endeavour.

Higher in the sky, and behind *Sirius*, we find the tiny Constellation of **Canis Minor**, the Lesser dog, and again it has but one star of importance: *Procyon*, α Canis Minoris, at 25°35' **(Cancer)**, 1°7' **Cancer**. Another very bright star, Vis. Mag. 0.48, *Procyon* is sometimes called the Northern Sirius.

The name Procyon, however, is that of the navigator and steersman of the ship Argo, whose crew made the epic voyage in search of the Golden Fleece – the quest for the true knowledge, the 'gold' of the alchemist, the knowledge of our origins, of what happened to make us as we now are, that knowledge which we have always felt deep down will heal us and take us forward to heights of attainment beyond anything we can imagine now.

Procyon never steered his companions to that goal in life, for Man was not then ready to find it, but in the heavens, those realms of the psyche where mortal time is no barrier to achievement, he is still getting us there. Here in mortal life new searchers, new teachers, new navigator-steersmen come among us in their turns, take us further along the road while they are with us, then join *Procyon* beyond mortal life to inspire us still.

Not all of them live and die dramatically like the Jesus or Giordano Bruno figures. Many are known only to friends and in their local communities, though the potential for wider recognition is always there if *Procyon* be strong and well aspected in their horoscopes.

If the aspects with the strength are less easy, then they may face *something* of the opposition that was turned on Jesus and Bruno, especially jealousy or envy from others, this star being so close to the twins *Castor* and *Pollux*, but in general this star does show one who uses its Mercury-Mars nature to dig deeply for knowledge and give freely of what is found.

Our remaining two Dogs are those of **Canes Venatici**, the *Hunting Dogs*. They can be called recent arrivals among us, for this small Constellation, ahead of Boötes and under the tail of the Great Bear, was introduced by the Polish astronomer Jan (Johannes) Hevelius in 1690 A.D. He counted 23 stars in his tiny new figure, and one of his colleagues made it 88 (!), with two galaxies and a fine globular cluster as well, but only two stars and one galaxy are commonly noticed with good eyesight.

First of these is *Asterion*, β Can. Ven., a very bright star but 30 light years away, reducing its vis. Mag. to 4.3. It is sometimes given the name *Chara*, but that is mythologically the name of the other of Diana's two dogs, that is, α Ca. Ve., the star which the astronomer Sir Edmund Halley (of comet fame) named *Cor Caroli*, Heart of Charles, to honour his king, Charles II.

But it was this star, α, which Hevelius himself named *Chara*, leader of the two dogs. When one sees such confusion enter the scene right at the inception of a constellation, one can only marvel that there is such amazing consistency about the more ancient figures in the sky.

Just to clear that up in summary:

β is *Asterion*, at 18°3' **(Virgo)**, 23°29' **Leo**.

α is *Chara* (or *Cor Caroli*) at 24°35' **(Virgo)**, 0°1' **Virgo**. But we may see the second name wrongly applied to the first of those.

The third item, less easily visible, is the 'Whirlpool Galaxy', M51, above the two dogs and appearing in some illustrations as the leash by which Bootes holds them. Unlike the dogs themselves, this Galaxy did attract attention in earlier times, being then called *Copula*, a Thong or Leash, as though anticipating the role it was to play later in history.

Copula is almost exactly conjunct with *Chara*, *Cor Caroli*, being at 24°39' **(Virgo)**, 0°5' **Virgo**, so we must take Ptolemy's Moon-Venus simile for it, unique in his listings, to apply to both the galaxy and the star. We might suppose from this very feminine and peaceable simile that Diana or Boötes must have the dogs out for an afternoon stroll, rather than for hunting, but its reputation in astrology is certainly more potent than that, and, as usual, not very auspicious.

Like *Alkaid* only two degrees beyond it, *Copula* often signifies a potential for taking public office, but there is certainly a note of misfortune if the holder allows Moon-Venus to symbolise the making of quick personal fortune from it. Nothing in **(Virgo)** permits that kind of corruption without penalty. But, excluding that temptation, *Copula* and *Alkaid* (and *Labrum*, between the two) can signify great respect given to the individual for services well given.

The same must, of course, apply to *Chara, Cor Caroli*, on

the same degree, and also to *Asterion* which fills in nicely a gap between *Mizar (Mirza)* and *Denebola*, with the same Saturn-Venus qualities.

CHAPTER 25

Man and Serpents

Man, with his forward-facing eyes, some five feet above the ground, must always feel vulnerable to a creature which crawls at the level of his feet. And being more defenceless than usual when in the water, he naturally has some fear also of creatures whose natural habitat is there. So he is not very fond of snakes, especially water-snakes.

Yet his mythology shows a very high regard for serpents, even while condemning them. They represent knowledge, and time, and eternity, all at once. 'Be wise as serpents', said Jesus to his disciples. The genus of creatures which is longest in proportion to its other dimensions is symbolic of our own (and all else's) extension four-dimensionally in time. The symbol of a snake devouring its own tail characterises eternity for us. A pair of them twining around a rod symbolises healing and wisdom, the Caduceus of medical profession, and now looks like an uncanny early intuition of the DNA molecule from which we know living forms to be built. A dream of several snakes eating their tails inspired the German scientist Benz to produce the formula which gave us our first petrol.

Greatest story of all, of course, is that of the serpent in the Garden of Eden, giving Eve, and then Adam, access to the Tree of the Knowledge of Good and Evil, starting us all on the road to equality with the gods. So now let us looks at some celestial snakes.

1. Hydra, the Water-Snake

In a large, rather empty-looking region above **Leo**, is just one bright star, *Alphard*, to mark this otherwise very faint Constellation. It is only 3° short of Regulus, for which it may be mistaken when conditions are not clear enough to see all the stars one would wish.

The name comes from the Arabic Al Fard Al Shujah, the Lone Star in the Snake, and the Arabs often dropped the watery connotation from the title of the Constellation itself. Their other name for it was *Al Hayya*, still meaning snake, but a word used much more than Shujah in telling the story of the Garden of Eden.

It makes good sense, however, to retain the water connection, for that whole story is about bringing Man out of the unconscious, oceanic state, a mere animal slave of 'the gods', to develop and use the intellect which was latent in him. The story of Eden still remains very controversial, and there are many who say that it would read differently if the serpent, rather than the 'other side', had won the day there.

There is indeed much to suggest that the association of the Serpent with the 'Devil', or 'Iblis', or 'Satan' was a smear-tactic by the forces against human development, rather than the truth. The whole symbol of the snake with its long body is very much about finding out the truth behind that myth or legend.

Alphard, with its Saturn-Venus planetary simile, surely must be about that meeting of The Bringer of Wisdom with Eve. Its proximity to *Regulus*, star of human glory among its own kind, must surely put our prime star of the Water-Snake into the role of the herald of 'the Ascent of Man', to borrow Bronowski's excellent phrase. And that is just what *Alphard*, α Hydrae, does symbolise on the horoscope. There is the ability to grow and to rise to high places, with always that Saturnine note of precaution, that we must be clear about much we know in objective truth about the matter, and that we endanger ourselves by letting a little knowledge and power go to our heads (which is really precisely where it does *not* go when we become besotted with power!) *Alphard's* present position is 27° **(Leo)**, 2°32' **Leo**.

2. Ophiuchus and Serpens

In our times, these are two separate Constellations, virtually three, in fact, for **Serpens** is itself in two parts, with **Ophiuchus** between them. But that is an astronomers' convenience only, and we are concerned more with the intimate relation of the 'Serpent Handler' with the snake that is twined about him, all the way from its head in his outstretched left hand to the tail at arm's length in the other.

Who was *Ophiuchus?* There are many answers in many ages, all showing us a highly skilled, hardworking doctor. The highly intuitive King James I of England (James VI to Scots) associated the figure with 'The Great Mediciner', Aesculapius. And many others have agreed with him, even saying that the rod about which the snakes of the Caduceus are wrapped is in reality a man being at once afflicted and healed by the representatives of Time and Knowledge. The one snake is usually drawn in black, darkness, the other in white, light.

Aesculapius, and the name does have a linguistic connection with Ophiuchus, was taught the healing arts by Apollo and Chiron, and he became the ship's doctor to the Argonauts during their search for the golden fleece. It seems that in some sense he actually found it, for later he became a healer extraordinary, much like the later Jesus, able even on occasion to restore life to the dead, as he did for King Hippolytus. But his attempt to revive Orion alarmed the gods once too often, and they removed him from this life forthwith.

Well, that's one way to explain his passing from our midst. A more positive outlook would be to see that he lives on to inspire his followers with his remarkable Divine gifts, rather than to have kept them in just his one pair of mortal hands. And it is the transmission of those abilities to heal that his Sign and Constellation is all about. We are not here speaking just symbolically, or idolatrously of 'the power of stars, or gods', but of inspiration which we may receive from a human soul that really has lived and practised among us here. The stars that symbolise him will show what we may do with what we may receive.

Our first star is at 21°47' **(Scorpio)**, 27°19' **Libra**, and it is *Unukhalhai* (pr. Oonookh Al Hay), the Neck of the Snake. The neck, rather than the head, is where a snake has its brain, its seat of knowledge. So this star is all about that knowledge that the good doctor has won from his labours, that knowledge of where we came from, what we are, where we are going, what holds us back, what to do about healing it.

This Saturn-Mars star, α Serpentis, does in some measure merit the black reputation it has gained from the debasers of astrology, for those who will abuse and, mis-use, the gifts available here are as deserving of being struck off the register as any corrupt doctor. But those who will give service, in healing or teaching of what they receive, have only good fortune to expect where Unukhalhai shines on them.

This half of the snake, by the way, to the man's left, is now called **Serpens Caput**, Head (side) of the Snake, counted a different constellation from **Serpens Cauda**, the Tail side, on the man's right.

Now we move into the stars of the man himself, with *Yed Prior* δ Ophiuchi, a linguistic hybrid of Arabic and Latin meaning the Fore Star of the Hand, and of course this hand is holding the snake near its head. *Yed Posterior*, rear star of the hand, is too close here to be sensibly taken separately. These stars and the previous one are (by longitude) either side of the main stars of **Centaurus**, symbol of the healer Chiron, which we have yet to discuss, but the meaning for us now is a shift from the knowledge gained with *Unukhalhai*, to putting it to use through this healing hand. Its Saturn-Venus quality is perfectly fitted to the purpose, and it is the sure Sign of the practical healer by hand when it is well placed and aspected on the horoscope. Its position is 2°4' **(Sagittarius)**, 8°22' **Scorpio**.

Han is our next star. ζ Ophiuchi, an unfortunate choice of name since it comes from old political Chinese astrology, nothing to do with our system. *Rukba*, the Knee, is where it is, but the title has not often been used. With its Saturn-Venus simile, it continues the theme of putting the knowledge to useful purpose, and hints at added strength from the promixity of *Antares* within the same degree. The position is now 9°3' **(Sagittarius)**, 15°22' **Scorpio**.

Sabik, η Oph., on the Doctor's other knee, is a word meaning Preceding, probably to indicate that this knee is ahead of the other. By longitude it is in very strong position, with the Head stars of Hercules and Ophiuchus before and after it respectively. It continues the Saturn-Venus theme on to 17°50' **(Sagittarius)**, 24°9' **Scorpio**.

Rasalhague, α Oph., derived from Al Ras Al Hawwa, is the Head of the Snake Handler, also meaning '—of the Snake *Charmer*', with the implication that this Doctor is not fighting with the creature, but actually has control *over* it. Since this is his Head star, the note is one of control by the mind, not by the brute strength that is so often evident in illustrations. The Saturn-Venus theme is still with us, now at 22°16' **(Sagittarius)**, 28°35' **Scorpio**.

Last important star of **Ophiuchus** is *Sinistra*, ν Oph., and simply the Latin for *left (hand)*, holding the tail of the snake. Our Saturn-Venus theme of intelligence and healing has now reached the formidable degree of 29° 34' **(Sagittarius)**, 5°53' **Sagittarius**.

3. Hercules and Draco

The Giant *Hercules* is of course famed for his legendary 'Labours', and his name is a bye-word for great strength. For all that fame his history is rather obscure, for his Greek biographers seem to have come upon him quite late in the day. There is a deep symbol in this figure confronting the huge Dragon, *Draco*, actually above the head of Ophiuchus in his contest with a more modest snake, even if pictures of the latter do show a creature that would swallow an ox for a snack! It seems that *Hercules* is engaged in a still greater contest and since, China apart, dragons are regarded as symbols of evil, we should not be surprised to find that *Hercules* and *Draco* have origins as far back as the Chaldean myth of the Sun-god Izhdubar (alias Gilgamesh) slaying the dragon Tiamat, with the help of the first of the Centaurs, Ea Bani.

This story has all the ring of the Fall of Phaethon about it – what else can the Dragon represent? – and of the Saviour of the World, and the Son of Man, in the forms of Gilgamesh/ Hercules, and Ea Bani (Son of Ea) respectively. The latter, still associated with the First Centaur, Chiron, has come right through to the Christ figure of our present times. The long-held place of St. George the dragon-slayer in Christian lore is also much to the point here.

So that is the ancient knowledge held by the serpentine monster *Draco*, and which *Hercules* is wresting from it. It is the same that the good Doctor beneath him is grappling with, but at a more profound level. Since it is perhaps a story accessible to fewer of us, at least until now, there are fewer major stars to mark it in us.

The first of these is *Rastaban*, the Dragon's Head, β Draconis, at 11°34' **(Sagittarius)**, 17°53' **Scorpio**, another Saturn-Venus star to keep up the healing theme of Serpens and Ophiuchus. The implication is that: Open up *this* head full of knowledge, and we really do have the key to our ills and the healing of them.

Next is *Ras Algethi*, 'Head of the Kneeler', since that is how Hercules is fighting his battle, though some think the title was once *Ras Aljauzi*, 'Head of the Giant'. Somehow the less exotic title seems the better to encourage us non-giants to take part, for we can all kneel. This star, α Herculis, shares the Saturn-Venus simile again, and is at 15°55' **(Sagittarius)**, 22°14' **Scorpio**.

We are back to the Dragon again for *Etamin*, γ Draconis, the name being another Arabic form of The Dragon's Head. The planetry simile is changed here, however, to Mars-Moon. Since both this star and its namesake *Rastaban* are commonly regarded as the two Eyes in the Head, there may be something here of the old notion that one's right eye sees good, the left eye evil. Mars-Moon is never popular as a combination in astrology, for it often does show the inclination to look on the black side of things. We are here looking perhaps at the source of that morbid tendency in us, with the strength of Hercules to slay it for us. In those who do overcome their own states of anxiety, revealed by Mars-Moon, there is always the power to heal others also. *Etamin* is at 27°42' **(Sagittarius)**, 4°1' **Sagittarius**

There we must leave the healing world of terrifying serpents and their brave slayers and tamers. For those among us blessed with the strength shown by these stars on their horoscopes. the terror is no worse than their first visits as students to the operating theatre, feeling worse then than the patient before them, but destined to become our healers in their maturity.

CHAPTER 26

The Argonauts

Everyone, almost, likes adventure stories: Jason and his fellow Argonauts are an evergreen in popular Greek mythology. But this is really a far more profund myth than mere adventure on the high seas.

Those who sailed in the ship *Argo* are now commemorated by one of the largest Constellations in the southern hemisphere of our skies. So large is it that in the past two centuries it has been split for the convenience of astronomers into three parts: **Vela**, the Sail, **Puppis**, the Poop, or Stern, and **Carina**, the Well, or Hull of the ship.

Under Captain Jason, and with Procyon, whom we've already met, as their navigator, the Argonauts went in search of the Golden Fleece. But not all who read the story today have much idea of what that object of their quest really signifies.

It amounts to this. The fleece of a sheep was once a unit of currency, as also were such measures as a bushel of wheat, a cubit of cedar, and so on. None of these, however, were currency such as one might hoard indefinitely, like sterling or dollars today. To have any value, they had to be passed on as payment while still fresh and usable for food or clothing. they were all ephemeral in their value, unlike gold, which lasted for ever.

The Golden Fleece, however, was something that combined or united the ephemeral with the eternal. And it came from a living creature, so it combined the inanimate of the material with the life of the spiritual worlds. The quest for that fleece was another enterprise like the search to re-enter Eden, and this time to eat of that forbidden Tree of Life. Man is made to live for ever, so ran the argument; he was only prevented from gaining his birthright by a god who feared the potential of an immortal race that would yet prove superior to himself.

And that has been always the true quest of the Alchemist, hide it as he might behind a display of making chemical gold from chemical lead. The real gold is himself as he intends to become, the gold that he already is, if he can but purify himself to be free of all the contaminants in his body, soul and mind, Salt, Sulphur and Mercury, as he terms them for disguise of his intent.

And of course it can be done and it is human destiny to do it, whether by pestle and crucible, or by prayer and fasting, or by exploring the Earth and the Heavens, or in the Life Hereafter. One thing is sure. It is no easy quest, but requires great effort, and faith in its worth if that effort is to be sustained. There is none among us that should deride or condemn another's chosen way of taking his place on *Argo's* deck. Now that we know what we are looking for, let's find it among the Living Stars.

Canopus, α star of **Carina** the hull, and once the α of the whole ship, is a truly brilliant sight, Vis. Mag. 0.86, but 53° below the Equator. Honoured by Ptolemy with a Saturn-Jupiter simile the name has two probable origins: first, Canopus, or Kanobos, was the chief navigator of the Greek fleet that sacked Troy, 1183 B.C., and who died near

Alexandria, Egypt, some years later. A monument was erected to him there, and in fact a town was renamed after him. The site is close to present Aboukir, scene of famous naval battles ever since. In due course, it is said, it was Ptolemy who named the great star in **Argo** after him also.

But a still earlier source for the name is the Coptic-Egyptian *Kahi-Nub*, Golden Earth, with a truly alchemical connotation. And with this star practically on the centreline of **(Cancer)**, 14°51' (20°23' **Gemini**), and conjunct with the wondrous Sirius, what better hope of the mastery of Life can one ask than to have these two promising symbols well placed and aspected on one's horoscope. Only let it not be forgotten that the quest for the Golden Fleece is still an arduous journey, even for those who will actually find it. Not all the stars together can bestow it without the questor earning it for him or her self.

The Quest finds another indicator of will to attain it at 28°19' **(Virgo)**, 3°51' **Virgo** where we have star *Markeb*. Note the 'e' in the spelling here; it is all that distinguishes it from the star of the same name, but spelt with an 'a' in Pegasus. *Markeb* is K Velae, in the Sail of the ship, and far enough north to be seen from Rome or New York late in March each year. With Vis. Mag. 2,63, it is rather a 'poor man's' Canopus, but still accorded the status of Saturn-Jupiter by Ptolemy. Its Virgoan placing puts the emphasis more on the spiritual nature of the quest, especially as it is close to *Zaniah* with that star's religious associations. So, that approach, along with a life of devoted service to others,is likely to be the voyage for those with *Markeb* prominent on their charts.

Third star *Foramen*, η Carinae finds us in the hull again, at 22°2' **(Libra)**, 27°24' **Virgo**. Again it is a Saturn-Jupiter, but its very variable magnitude, anything between a glaring 1 and a dim 7, gives it a very Libran quality: tomorrow I will; today I won't bother; yesterday it seemed like a good idea . . . It is, however, close in longitude to wonderful *Spica*, so the appeal to take up the quest is definitely there. Of the three stars we have used to explore with the Argonauts, *Foramen*, mut rank second in importance, lacking the brilliance of *Canopus* but, like the latter, having the best of company by conjunction. The name *Foramen* means a Hole (in Latin), possibly because it is not visible at all to normal eyes when its magnitude goes down to 7.

We could fill a whole book with the vast Constellation of **Argo**, but the art of good seership is to know when one has seen Signs enough.

CHAPTER 27

The Cross, The Crown and the Centaur

Centaurus is a huge Constellation which reaches from nearly overhead at our South Pole right up to the zenith over North Africa. It is also a very old one, perhaps as old as the Zodiacal Sign **Sagittarius**, of such similar imagery. It is not difficult for a newcomer to astronomy or astrology to confuse the one with the other, for their associations are so similar.

In recent times, however, a distinction has grown up for those who are sensitive to meaning in the heavens, and this seems to have spread especially since the discovery of the little planet *Chiron* in 1977.

The Zodiacal Sign, **Sagittarius**, has long been associated with higher learning, philosophy, human progress, religion, life hereafter, and God, but always with a taint of the old paganism where the deity was more Jupiter, the god, than the real Divinity. And the centaur by which the Constellation is illustrated, was often called simply the Archer, the emphasis being on his warlike prowess rather than his finer qualities as the educator and raiser of humanity. The Southerly Constellation, **Centaurus**, not being of the Zodiac, was barely noticed at all, especially by the majority of astrologers, who used few if any of the 'fixed stars', as they liked to call our living heavens.

The centaurs of Sagittarius, however, are traditionally a wild lot, and they threw out the one among them who wanted to use his great power and intelligence to teach and aid mankind. He, *Chiron*, went his way, rejected by his own, a master not without honour save in his own country. He was mortally wounded but, having attained the Mastery of Life, he could not die. And so he taught the heroes among men, and some of the gods too, the knowledge that could raise them to the Divine quality that was/is their ultimate destiny.

The figure is familiar of course: Buddha, Isaiah, Jesus, Muhammad; name a great avatar or prophet and it is he – or she. No Zodiac Sign has ever described one, nor any star nor planet, not until the finding of *Chiron*, that 'little child', among planets which many still refuse to recognise as a valid part of our reading and reckoning: 'It is an asteroid', 'a planetoid', 'a burnt-out comet'; it is rejected by those who, like Caiaphas of old, say: 'See to it that no new prophet ariseth among us.'

Surely if any figure in our history deserves a Sign by which we may recognise him in the heavens, it is that ever-returning mentor at critical moments of our growth and transformation. And **Centaurus** is surely that Sign, brilliant and expansive to cover more than half the planet.

Three stars are enough for now to show us where we and this cast-out friend from the centaurs have something to share. The first of these is α Crucis, *Acrux*, prime star of the **Southern Cross**, **Crux**, which is featured on the flags of Australia and New Zealand. It is a fine star of Vis. Mag. 1.05, accorded the appropriate simile Jupiter by Ptolemy. He, by the way, could see it from northern Egypt with an ease not possible now, for precession has carried **Centaurus**, of which **Crux** was long an integral part, farther to the south in our skies.

At 11°40' **(Scorpio)**, 17°12' **Libra**, **Acrux** is significantly conjunct by longitude, all save 12' of arc, with *Alphecca*, prime star of **Corona Borealis**, the Northern Crown which lies close to the head of **Boötes** in our more familiar skies. We may not see The Cross from here but we can see the Crown that comes as the reward for carrying it a little of the way. *Alphecca's* name comes from 'Bright One of the Bowl' for in fact the Crown is that way up in the sky.

If that sounds a little bit too 'Christian Establishment' for some tastes, remember that there is *no* prophet in history that has not suffered persecution for bringing new light to peoples when many of them felt more comfortable in their familiar half-darkness.

The next star we consider is β Centauri, *Agena*, the lovely Venus-Jupiter star, Vis. Mag. 0.86, at 23°34' **(Scorpio)**, 29°6' **Libra**. The name's origin is lost in antiquity but it has the alternative Arabic name *Hadar*, from the word in that tongue for the Ground or Earth, a vital element, because it is the field of action for the high spiritual ideals that are manifest in all the stars we are now looking at.

Close to that is α Centauri, actually three stars very close to each other as we see them, and one of them actually the closest visible star to us in real distance, a mere 4¼ light years, so that it is called *Proxima Centauri*. More generally, however, α as a whole is called *Rigel Kentaur*, Foot of the Centaur. Another name for it is *Bungula*, again meaning Foot if we remove the inexplicable 'B' from it. Yet a third name is *Tolliman*, mentioned here only because readers may find it in the odd book or so. Given Venus-Jupiter acclaim by Ptolemy, this much admired star trio is at 29°17' **(Scorpio)**, 4°49' **Scorpio**.

Whoever has any or all of these stars prominent in the horoscope will be noted for great enthusiasm for whatever causes they embrace and they are likely to be quite self-sacrificing about it. They can even afford that expenditure if the stars are well aspected, for they truly do indicate a bountiful flow of energies from within, or Above, however we may express it. The author's ex-wife, now good friend and companion, has *Agena* strong, and apart from greatly encouraging the writing of this volume, retains the youthfulness to outrun many a bus that failed to stop for her, and devotes herself to rigorous yoga that leaves him fearful that she may ask him to try it too!

CHAPTER 28

Auriga the Charioteer

Above the stars of **Orion** is the rhomboidal shape which we know as The Wagoner or, more usually, as the Charioteer. The choice depends on how one finds it illustrated, with oxen or horses. It is a very old Constellation, pre-Babylonian, but the mythology behind it is now too obscure to be sure about it. The notion that it may have connection with the Chariot card of the Tarot is by no means unreasonable, for that method of divination, once said to have originated in our own medieval centuries, is actually very much older indeed.

Several of the stars can be easily seen on a clear night but two in particular attract attention. *Capella*, α Aurigae, takes its name from a quite different source, for it means the Little She-Goat. It is very bright and cheerful to see, with a Vis. Mag. of 0.21, at a position of 21°39' **(Gemini)**, 27°11' **Taurus**. Its Mars-Mercury designation, like that of longitudinally neighbouring *Bellatrix* below it, shows up that same will to 'have a go', and calls for the same pause for thought to be sure what one is actually taking on. In the Tarot, the Chariot often denotes the same note of impulsiveness which, while not saying that the consulter is necessarily going the wrong way, still counsels caution and objective second thoughts.

Menkalinan, β Aurigae, at 29°44' **(Gemini)**, 5°16' **Gemini**, takes its name from the Arabic for The Shoulder of the Rein-holder (i.e. The Driver of the Chariot), and it has the same Mars-Mercury styling as our previous entry. And it too is conjunct with, but above a shoulder star of **Orion**, the other shoulder, *Betelgeuz* this time, also a Mars-Mercury. What we said for *Capella*, therefore, can be said again at this point eight degrees farther along.

CHAPTER 29

Crater the Chalice

One star is all that concerns us in **Crater**, the *Chalice*, or *Goblet*, or *Cup* (not a crater of the volcanic or bombardment kind, please). It is a small southerly Constellation whose prime star at the bottom of the vessel has escaped attention here in the north, because it is effectively conjunct in longitude with the star we can see more easily, at the rim or lip of the cup. The vessel is sometimes associated with the Chalice of the Last Supper, not unreasonably since the vessel is in the general vicinity of **Centaurus**, but more traditionally it is the Goblet owned by Apollo, the Sun-God, the latter being very possibly the name of our second sun before that one exploded to become known to us as Phaethon. So perhaps this Chalice does have a note of doom about it, Christian or earlier.

But that tinge of sorrow is, after all, the precursor to a moment of glory for the Prince of Peace, Jesus or any other before or since his time, and so it is not a surprise that Ptolemy rates *Labrum*, the star at the Lip of the Cup, as a

Venus-Mercury type. At 26°14' **(Virgo)**, 1°46' **Virgo**, it is effectively conjunct with *Alkaid* and should thus suggest to such bearers of office the familiar line from Shakespeare: 'In Peace there's nothing so becomes a man, as modest stillness and humility.'

CHAPTER 30

The Lyre and the Swan

Profound and popular though the myth of Orpheus and Euridice is, only one small Constellation is unquestionably associated with it: **Lyra**, the tragic musician's Lyre.

It is marked in the sky by the magnificnt star *Vega*, sometimes Wega, with a Vis. Mag. of 0.14, and wonderfully clear to see at 15°9' **(Capricorn)**, 20°41' **Sagittarius**.

It also marks one corner of Patrick Moore's very fine introduction to the figures of the night sky, *The Summer Triangle*. The other corners of this large, easily recognised summertime sight are *Altair*, in Aquila the Eagle, and *Deneb Adige* in the tail of Cygnus the Swan, second of our subjects in this chapter.

Whatever other troubles Orpheus may have had, he was certainly popular for his music, and popularity with one's fellows is what *Vega* marks on a horoscope if it is the least bit well aspected. It is a Venus-Mercury star, and the only note of caution to go with it is to remember that popularity is a tool for living happily and honestly with one's fellow beings, not shamelessly exploiting their welcome.

Cygnus, the Swan, is said by some to be Orpheus himself, though the Arabs rate it only as a hen (and what's wrong with that?). Truly, though, it looks only like a swan in full flight, huge wings at full stretch, long neck and head reaching far in front. It is a joy to look at on a fine night and count how many of its numerous stars one can see and name.

Only two concern us here, though: *Albireo*, the Beak, β Cygni, being the first of them, at 1°6' **(Aquarius)**, 6°38' **Capricorn**. It is a Venus Mercury star, in keeping with *Vega*, and it would be difficult to think of a better start to the social Sign of **(Aquarius)**. Well aspected people really do soar to great heights on this one and, being well aspected people, of course they behave appropriately when they get there. If not, however, they have been known to be shot down again!

Deneb Adige, Tail of the Hen, but Swan to us, is α Cygni, at 4°49' (**Pisces)**, 10°21' **Aquarius**, and another Venus-Mercury beauty. The emphasis here is rather more on the Mercury, for this is conjunct by longitude with the star of Gabriel the Announcing Angel, *Fomalhut*.

CHAPTER 31

An Archangel, a Fish and Three Birds

Columba, The Dove, in our southern skies, is another of the newer Constellations, introduced in the 17th Century A.D. It is sometimes called Noah's Dove, **Columba Noae**. One star alone is prominent, the α of the figure, its name *Phact*, from an Arabic word for Earth, which long predates its inclusion in **Columba**. *Phact* is a Venus-Mercury star, as we should hope for in a Dove but actually a remarkable piece of premonition by Ptolemy! At 21°42' **(Gemini)**, 27°14' **Taurus**, it may be seen as exercising a moderating influence on the Mars-Mercury *Capella*, with which it is nearly conjunct.

Corvus, the Crow, or Raven, is an early Constellation with an amusing story to it. Apollo sent Corvus out with Crater the Cup to get some water. Corvus, however, took time off to have a snack of figs and, as an excuse for the delay, he brought back Hydra the Water Snake and blamed him. Apollo didn't believe a word of it, and promptly put bird, cup and snake all together in the sky, out of mischief for ever. Well, it's as believable as Jack and Jill, I suppose.

Only δ Corvi, *Algorab*, 'The Crow', matters much to us. It is a Mars-Saturn star at 13°12' **(Libra)**, 18°44' **Virgo**, and can indeed show up the more troublesome side of Libra, a variation on the truth when an excuse looks to be safer, but is not always found to be so – as the Crow discovered. Not a significant star when well aspected, but can be a nuisance if aspects or planets involved are hard ones.

Our final bird is **Aquila**, the Eagle, with two stars to offer us. The eagle has seen so much usage as a standard symbol for communities everywhere that, apart from having its origins in the Middle East in this case, we can say nothing specific about it.

First of the two stars is *Altair*, α Aquilae, at 1°34' **(Aquarius)** 7°6' **Capricorn**, a Mars-Jupiter type as one would expect for the star whose name means Eagle. Even traditionalists usually like this one; there is no controversy raised when we note that it usually does show up good respect from one's fellow beings, so long as it is well placed. If it is not, the owner of the chart may be one of those who drops things upon others from a great height. He can be sure he will not go on forever doing that.

Second star is *Deneb Aquilae*, Tail of the Eagle, at 19°37' **(Capricorn)**, 25°9' **Sagittarius**, a Mars-Jupiter like its companion. The difference in interpretation usually observed is less inclination to glare down upon one's underlings, as in that first flush of promotion, a more assured feel for the job, and a better reputation thus gained in whatever office one holds. Negatively there may be that slight lack of effort needed to achieve something that really should be an easy target.

And now for the **Archangel Gabriel**, whose star, as we have said more than once in various parts of this book, is the prime star of the Southern fish α **Piscis Australis**, the Mouth of the fish: *Fomalhut*. It is of Venus-Mercury nature, at 3°30' **(Pisces)**, 9°2' **Aquarius**. For all its exalted association, this star has often been counted a malefic, especially in mundane and political affairs. Really, if we take the angelic significance seriously, we should not be too surprised at occasional celestial indignation over some of our viler projects for destroying life around us.

On the personal horoscope, however, *Fomalhut* shows up a good talent and a ready will to speak out when necessary, and to contribute new ideas and thinking when they are most needed. If not so well aspected, there can be a tendency to 'speak with the tongues of angels, yet be but an empty sounding brass', as St. Paul put it.

And on that note we have completed our round of the Zodiac and its family of closer neighbours.

Table of Star Data
for January 1989

Notes on using this Table
The First column gives the star's most familiar name first, followed by alternative names.

Column Two gives the astronomers' Greek letter designation, and the Constellation to which the star belongs. The grammar of the Latin has been dispensed with, so as to make the Constellation's name clearer, and as the same will be found in the Index.

Column Three shows the visual Magnitude, the apparent brightness of the star, chiefly to give a clue as to how easily or not a star may be seen in the sky. A Vis. Mag. of more than 4 is usually very difficult to see, and even 3 is not easy for older eyes.

Column Four gives the planetary simile according to Ptolemy. If this appears in (brackets), it is not his but our own estimate of what he would have given. The author has experimented sometimes with applying the outer planets also to Ptolemy's classifications, so that where he gives Saturn, we may say 'Saturn and/or Uranus'. The same applies to Mars-Pluto, and Jupiter-Neptune. We have also experimented with a 'house' reckoning, so that a Moon designation for a star in **(Sagittarius)** would be like Moon in a Sixth-House situation, this in addition to whatever house of the horoscope the star is in, since Moon has its nominal First House in its Home Sign, **(Cancer)**. This data has not been put into the Table, but some readers may like to try it out.

Column Five shows where the star will be located astrologically on a horoscope drawn by the normal, *tropical*, zodiac.

Column Six gives the 'Orb of Effect' according to most opinions today, and this is counted to either side of the position. For example, if the position is 8°54' **(Aries)**, and the orb is 2°10', then, a planet may be reckoned as 'on' that star if it is between 6°44' and 11°4' of **(Aries)**. Beyond those limits the conjunction is weak, and should be discounted altogether at more than 1° outside them. Few astrologers reckon a star effective in any aspect but conjunction, or sometimes opposition, but the few who work also with semi-sextiles, sextiles, squares, trines and quincunxes, can claim the support of the great William Lilly in this. In that case they should apply the same example as just given, but of course in the sign where the planet is.

Column Seven shows how far in zodiacal longitude a star will shift its position in 10 years. The unit used is Minutes of Arc. Thus the star shown at 8°54' **(Aries)** for January 1989, having a 10-yr shift of 6.9 Minutes, was at 8°47' in 1979, and will be at 9°1' in 1999.

Column Eight is for those who use Sidereal Astrology, that is by the zodiacal Constellations where they are actually to be seen in the sky now, rather than by the long-established locations of the *signs*. Most astrologers may ignore this column apart from interest's sake.

Column Nine gives the declination of the star above (North) or below (South) the Earth's Equator,or the Celestial Equator as it is called when extended out to infinity. This is the up-down reference system most used by astronomers and astrologers alike, if used at all.

But Column Ten gives the same North-South 'Celestial Latitude' above and below the Ecliptic, our path round the Sun, for those who, like this author, find that more meaningful to them.

Star Data Table
January 1989

Abbreviations, Cols, 5 and 8: AR=Aries, TA=Taurus, GE=Gemini, CN=Cancer, LE=Leo, VI=Virgo, LI=Libra, SC=Scorpio, SA=Sagittarius, CP=Capricorn, AQ=Aquarius, PS=Pisces.

Example: 2 AR 19 = 2° 19′ Aries

Some long names have had to be abbreviated but should be clear.

Star Name(s)	**Constellation & Greek Letter**	**Vis. Mag.**	**Planet Simile**
Deneb Kaitos Difda	β Cetus	2.02	Saturn
Algenib	γ Pegasus	2.84	Mars–Mercury
Alpheratz	α Androm'a	2.06	Jupiter–Venus
Baten Kaitos	ζ Cetus	3.92	Saturn
Kullat Nuni Al Pherg	η Pisces	3.72	Saturn–Jupiter
Al Risha	α Pisces	4.7	
Androm, Galaxy Vertex	M31 Androm	3.70	Mars–Moon
Mirach	β Androm'a	2.02	Venus
Stella Mira	o Cetus	Var 2/10	(Mars–Saturn
Sharatan	β Aries	2.68	Mars–Saturn
Mesartim	γ Aries	4.6	Saturn–Mars
Hamal	α Aries	2.0	Mars–Saturn
Schedir	α Cassiop	2.47	(Mars–Jupiter)

Place by (Sign)	Orb of Effect	10 Yr Shift (Mins)	Sidereal Place	Declin-ation	Cel. Lat.
2 AR 19	2°10′	6.9	7 PS 51	18S45	20S46
8 AR 54	2°0′	7.0	14 PS 26	15N04	12N36
14 AR 03	2°10′	6.7	19 PS 35	28N58	25N41
21 AR 40	1°30′	7.4	27 PS 12	11 S 02	20S20
26 AR 38	1°30′	9.02	2 AR 10	15N15	5N22
Conjunct next entry					
27 AR 38	1°30′	8.02	3 AR 15	41N10	33N21
0 TA 13	2°10′	6.8	5 AR 45	35N31	25N56
1 TA 21	1°30′	7.3	6 AR 53	3S30	15S31
3 TA 48	2°0′	9.3	9 AR 20	20N43	8N29
4 TA 30	1°10′	6.0	10 AR 02	18N47	7N06
7 TA 28	2°10′	7.3	13 AR 0	23N22	9N58
7 TA 43	2°10′	5.6	13 AR 15	56N31	46N20

Star Name(s)	Constellation & Greek Letter	Vis. Mag.	Planet Simile
Acamar	θ Eridan'	3.8	(Jupiter)
Menkar	α Cetus	2.54	Saturn
Almach Alamak	γ Androm'a	2.14	Venus
Zaurak	γ Eridanus	3.19	(Saturn–Mars)
Capulus, Gyrus	M34 Pers's	4.0	Mars–Mercury
Algol	β Pers's	Var 2/2.3	Saturn–Jupiter
Alcyone	η Taurus	2.8	Moon–Mars
Prima Hyadum	γ Taurus	3.9	Saturn–Mercury
Ain Hyadum	ϵ Taurus	3.63	Mercury–Mars
Aldebaran Oculus Tauri	α Taurus	1.06	Mars
Cursa	β Eridanus	2.8	(Jupiter –Mercury)
Rigel, Rijl	β Orion	0.92	Jupiter –Mars

Place by (Sign)	Orb of Effect	10 Yr Shift (Mins)	Sidereal Place	Declin-ation	Cel. Lat.
8 TA 09	1°30′	4.5	13 AR 36	40S05	63S40
14 TA 06	2°0′	7.7	19 AR 38	4N01	12S35
14 TA 08	2°10′	7.1	19 AR 40	42N14	27N48
23 TA 22	1°40′	7.9	28 AR 54	14S03	32S29
24 TA 16	1°30′	10.34	29 AR 48	57N04	40N22
26 TA 08	2°0′	7.7	1 TA 40	40N53	22N25
29 TA 52	2°0′	8.0	5 TA 24	23N52	4N02
5 GE 37	1°30′	8.0	11 TA 09	15N26	5S44
8 GE 17	1°30′	8.0	13 TA 49	15N28	5S42
9 GE 36	2°30′	8.2	15 TA 08	16N21	5S28
15 GE 18	2°0′	8.0	20 TA 45	5S18	27S40
16 GE 32	2°40′	8.3	22 TA 04	8S18	31S08

Star Name(s)	Constellation & Greek Letter	Vis. Mag.	Planet Simile
Bellatrix	γ Orion	1.6	Mars–Mercury
Capella	α Auriga	0.21	Mars–Mercury
Phact	α Columba	2.75	Mars–Mercury
Mintaka	δ Orion	2.48	Saturn–Mercury
El Nath, Alkab	β Taurus	1.78	Mars
Ensis, Hatysa	i Orion	4.6	Mars–Moon
Al Nilam	ϵ orion	1.75	Jupiter –Saturn
Al Hecka	ζ Taurus	1.6	Mars
Saiph, Saif	χ Orion	2.06	(Mars–Saturn)
Polaris	α Ursa-Min	2.1	Saturn–Venus
Betelgeuz	α Orion	0.7	Mars–Mercury
Menkalinan	β Aurigae	1.8	Mars–Mercury

Place by (Sign)	Orb of Effect	10 Yr Shift (Mins)	Sidereal Place	Declin- ation	Cel. Lat.
20 GE 45	2°20′	8.3	26 TA 17	6N17	16S50
21 GE 39	2°40′	8.3	27 TA 11	45N55	22N55
21 GE 42	2°0′	8.3	27 TA 14	34S07	57S23
22 GE 08	2°10′	8.2	27 TA 40	0S21	23S37
22 GE 30	2°20′	8.3	28 TA 02	28N32	5N23
22 GE 48	1°20′	8.3	28 TA 20	5S26	28S42
23 GE 14	2°20′	8.3	28 TA 46	1S15	24S32
24 GE 35	2°20′	8.3	0 GE 07	21N06	2S12
26 GE 29	2°10′	8.2	1 GE 57	9S56	32S20
28 GE 22	2°10′	8.2	3 GE 54	88N53	66N05
28 GE 33	2°40′	8.4	4 GE 05	7N42	16S02
29 GE 44	2°20′	8.4	5 GE 16	44N56	21N30

Star Name(s)	**Constellation & Greek Letter**	**Vis. Mag.**	**Planet Simile**
Tejat Prior Tahat Al Awwal	η Gemini	3.2	Mercury –Venus
Dirah, Nuhaiti Tejat Posterior, Tahat Al Thani	μ Gemini	3.19	Mercury –Venus
Al Hena Al Maisan	γ Gemini	1.8	Mercury –Venus
Sirius, Suhail	α Canis-Maj	0.06	Jupiter –Mars
Canopus Kahi-Nub	α Carina	0.86	Saturn –Jupiter
Al Wasat	δ Gemini	3.52	Saturn
Propus	i Gemini	3.09	Mercury –Venus
Castor	α Gemini	1.58	Mercury
Pollux	β Gemini	1.16	Mars
Procyon	α Canis-Min	0.48	Mercury –Mars
Altarf	β Cancer	3.5	(Mars)
Praesaepe	M44 Cancer	5.22	Mars–Moon

Place by (Sign)	Orb of Effect	10 Yr Shift (Mins)	Sidereal Place	Declin-ation	Cel. Lat.
3 CN 16	1°40′	8.4	8 GE 50	22N32	0S54
5 CN 08	1°40′	8.4	10 GE 40	22N38	0S50
8 CN 57	2°20′	8.4	14 GE 29	16N28	6S45
13 CN 54	2°40′	8.2	19 GE 39	16S36	39S35
14 CN 51	2°40′	8.0	20 GE 23	52S39	75S50
18 CN 24	1°40′	8.9	23 GE 56	22N08	0S11
18 CN 52	1°40′	9.3	24 GE 24	27N57	5N45
20 CN 04	2°20′	8.2	25 GE 36	32N04	10N05
23 CN 02	2°30′	8.0	28 GE 34	28N13	6N40
25 CN 35	2°40′	8.1	1 CN 35	5N26	16S00
0 LE 35	1°40′	8.0	6 CN 0	8N31	9S51
7 LE 05	1°0′	8.6	12 CN 37	20N15	1N33

Star Name(s)	Constellation & Greek Letter	Vis. Mag.	Planet Simile
Nth Asellus	γ Cancer	4.73	Mars–Sun
Sth Asellus	δ Cancer	4.17	Mars–Sun
Kochab, Kakkab	β Ursa-Min	2.02	(Saturn Mercury)
Acubens	α Cancer	4.27	Saturn–Mercury
Dubb, Dubhe	α Urs-Maj	1.95	(Mercury –Venus)
Merak	β Urs-Maj	2.3	(Saturn–Mercury)
Al Genubi *Al Janubi Al Asad* *Asad Australis*	ϵ Leo	3.12	Saturn –Mars
Al Ashfar	μ Leo	4.3	(Saturn –Mars)
Alphard	α Hydra	1.98	Saturn –Venus
Adhafera	ζ Leo	3.65	Saturn–Mercury
Al Jabbah	η Leo	3.58	Saturn–Mercury

Place by (Sign)	Orb of Effect	10 Yr Shift (Mins)	Sidereal Place	Declin-ation	Cel. Lat.
7 LE 24	1°0′	8.6	12 CN 56	21N46	3N11
8 LE 34	1°30′	8.7	14 CN 06	18N27	0N04
12 LE 37	2°10′	7.0	18 CN 09	73N56	73N36
13 LE 27	1°30′	8.2	18 CN 59	12N10	5S05
14 LE 52	2°20′	5.5	20 CN 24	61N06	49N39
19 LE 19	2°10′	6.0	24 CN 51	55N49	45N03
20 LE 32	1°40′	7.4	26 CN 04	24N09	9N43
22 LE 30	1°10′	6.8	28 CN 02	18N36	15N04
27 LE 00	2°20′	7.4	2 LE 32	8S19	22S23
27 LE 23	1°30′	7.3	2 LE 55	23N49	11N52
27 LE 42	1°30′	7.4	3 LE 14	17N09	4N52

Star Name(s)	**Constellation & Greek Letter**	**Vis. Mag.**	**Planet Simile**
Al Geiba	γ Leo	2.58	Saturn–Mercury
Regulus Cor Leonis, Qalb Al Asad	α Leo	1.34	Mars–Jupiter
Al Phecda	γ Ursa-Maj	2.54	(Jupiter –Venus)
Alioth	ϵ Ursa-Maj	1.68	(Saturn –Venus)
Zosma, Dhur	δ Leo	2.58	Saturn –Venus
Mizar, Mirza, Alcor	ζ Ursa-Maj	2.4	(Saturn –Venus)
Asterion	β Canes-Venatici	4.3	(Saturn –Venus)
Denebola	β Leo	2.23	Saturn –Venus
Copula	M51 Canes-Venatici	6.0	Moon–Venus
Chara	α Canes-Venatici	2.9	Moon–Venus
Labrum	δ Crater	3.82	Venus–Mercury

Place by (Sign)	Orb of Effect	10 Yr Shift (Mins)	Sidereal Place	Declin-ation	Cel. Lat.
29 LE 17	2°10′	7.3	4 LE 49	19N41	9N05
29 LE 38	2°30′	7.4	5 LE 10	12N22	0N28
0 VI 09	2°0′	5.5	5 LE 40	52N43	47N00
8 VI 39	2°20′	4.7	14 LE 11	64N17	54N32
11 VI 04	2°0′	7.1	16 LE 36	20N58	14N20
15 VI 24	2°10′	4.5	20 LE 56	54N51	56N18
18 VI 03	1°30′	4.2	23 LE 28	41N34	40N33
21 VI 23	2°10′	7.6	26 LE 48	15N01	12N16
24 VI 39	1°0′	6.1	0 VI 10	47N36	50N55

This star is conjunct with *Chara*

Place by (Sign)	Orb of Effect	10 Yr Shift (Mins)	Sidereal Place	Declin-ation	Cel. Lat.
24 VI 39	2°0′	6.0	0 VI 10	37N43	44N20
26 VI 14	1°30′	5.7	1 VI 41	14S21	17S34

Star Name(s)	**Constellation & Greek Letter**	**Vis. Mag.**	**Planet Simile**
Al Kaid	η ursa-Maj	1.91	(Moon–Mercury)
Zavijava *Al Araf, Al Araph*	β Virgo	3.8	Mercury–Mars
Markeb	K Vela	2.63	Saturn–Jupiter
Zaniah	η Virgo	2.95	Mercury–Venus
Vindemiatrix *Al Muredin*	ϵ Virgo	2.95	Saturn–Mercury
Caphir *Porrima*	γ Virgo	2.91	Mercury–Venus
Al Gorab	δ Corvus	3.1	Mars–Saturn
Seginus	γ Bootes	3.23	Mercury–Saturn
Foramen	η Carina	Var 1/7	Saturn–Jupiter
Spica, Ishtar	α Virgo	0.9 (Var)	Venus–Mars
Arcturus	α Bootes	0.24	Mars–Jupiter

Place by (Sign)	Orb of Effect	10 Yr Shift (Mins)	Sidereal Place	Declin- ation	Cel. Lat.
26 VI 38	2°20′	5.2	2 VI 05	49N17	54N05
26 VI 56	1°30′	7.8	2 VI 21	2N13	0N42
28 VI 19	2°0′	4.6	3 VI 47	54S40	63S43
4 LI 34	1°40′	7.6	10 VI 01	0S13	1N22
9 LI 41	1°40′	7.0	15 VI 07	11N23	16N13
9 LI 54	1°40′	7.6	15 VI 19	1S01	2N48
13 LI 12	1°40′	6.9	18 VI 38	16S04	12S11
17 LI 13	1°40′	6.4	22 VI 40	38N39	49N33
22 LI 03	1°30′	4.1	27 VI 31	59S16	58S55
23 LI 36	2°40′	7.1	29 VI 02	10S45	2S03
23 LI 56	2°40′	6.8	29 VI 22	19N36	30N47

Star Name(s)	**Constellation & Greek Letter**	**Vis. Mag.**	**Planet Simile**
Izar	ϵ Bootes	2.7	(Saturn –Venus)
Princeps Tsieh Kung	δ Bootes	3.54	Mercury –Saturn
Khambalia	λ Virgo	4.6	Mercury –Mars
Al Ghafar, Syrma	i Virgo		
Acrux	α Crux	1.05	Jupiter
Al Phecca	α Corona-Borealis	2.31	Venus–Mercury
South Scale Zuben Al Genubi	α Libra	3.0	Jupiter –Mars
North Scale Zuben Al Shamali	β Libra	2.74	Jupiter –Mercury
Unukh Al Hai Col Serpentis	α Serpens	2.75	Saturn –Mars
Agena	β Centaurus	0.86	Venus–Jupiter
Rigel Centaurus Bungula, Tolliman	α Centaurus	0.06	Venus–Jupiter
Yed Prior	δ Ophiuchus	3.03	Saturn–Venus

Place by (Sign)	Orb of Effect	10 Yr Shift (Mins)	Sidereal Place	Declin-ation	Cel. Lat.
28 LI 20	2°0′	7.0	3 LI 45	29N27	40N38
2 SC 44	1°40′	7.0	8 LI 10	33N37	48N59
6 SC 40	1°10′	7.9	12 LI 05	13S00	0N28

Other data as *Khambalia*, with which it is cojunct.

Place by (Sign)	Orb of Effect	10 Yr Shift (Mins)	Sidereal Place	Declin-ation	Cel. Lat.
11 SC 40	2°30′	4.7	17 LI 08	62S39	52S52
11 SC 54	2°10′	7.3	17 LI 20	26N59	44N20
14 SC 53	1°40′	7.6	20 LI 19	15S43	0N20
19 SC 10	2°0′	7.8	24 LI 35	9S05	8N30
21 SC 46	2°0′	7.7	27 LI 12	6N41	25N25
23 SC 34	2°40′	6.4	29 LI 01	59S59	44S09
29 SC 17	2°40′	6.1	4 SC 44	60S30	42S34
2 SA 04	1°40′	8.0	8 SC 15	3S29	17N15

Star Name(s)	**Constellation & Greek Letter**	**Vis. Mag.**	**Planet Simile**
Isidis Dschubba (not Acrab)	δ Scorpio	2.54	Mars–Saturn
Graffias	β Scorpio	2.9	Mars–Saturn
Han Al Rukba	ζ Ophiuchus	2.7	Saturn –Venus
Antares Cor Scorpio Qalb Al Aqrab	α Scorpio	1.22 (Var)	Mars–Jupiter
Rastaban	β Draco	2.99	Saturn –Venus
Ras Al Gethi	α Hercules	3.84	(Saturn –Venus)
Sabik	η Ophiuchus	2.63	Saturn –Venus
Rasalhague	α Ophiuchus	2.14	Saturn –Venus
Lesath, Lesuth	u Scorpio	2.8	Mercury –Mars
Aculeus	M6 Scorpio	5.3	Mars–Moon
Etamin	γ Draco	2.42	(Mars–Moon)

Place by (Sign)	Orb of Effect	10 Yr Shift (Mins)	Sidereal Place	Declin-ation	Cel. Lat.
2 SA 20	2°0′	7.9	8 SC 32	22S24	1S58
3 SA 04	2°0′	7.9	9 SC 15	19S35	1N01
9 SA 03	2°0′	8.2	15 SC 15	10S24	11N24
9 SA 40	2°30′	8.1	15 SC 52	26S15	4S34
11 SA 33	1°40′	7.5	17 SC 46	53N22	75N17
15 SA 55	1°30′	8.0	22 SC 07	14N47	36N53
17 SA 50	2°0′	8.3	24 SC 02	15S38	7N12
22 SA 16	2°10′	8.3	28 SC 28	12N37	35N51
23 SA 50	2°0′	8.4	0 SA 02	37S14	14S00
25 SA 44	1°0′	8.3	1 SA 56	32S10	8S50
27 SA 42	2°10′	8.0	3 SA 54	51N44	75N00

Star Name(s)	**Constellation & Greek Letter**	**Vis. Mag.**	**Planet Simile**
Acumen	M7 Scorpio	7.4	Mars–Moon
Sinistra	ν Ophiuchus	3.03	Saturn –Venus
Spiculum Trifid Nebula	*M8, M20, M21 Sagittarius*	*5.0*	*Mars–Moon*
Polis	μ Sagittari	4.01	Jupiter –Mars
Kaus Borealis	λ Sagittari	2.94	(Mercury –Mars)
Facies	M22 Sagittari	5.0	Sun–Mars
Pelagus Nunki	σ Sagittari	2.14	Jupiter –Mercury
Ascella Axilla	ζ Saggitari	2.71	Jupiter –Mercury
Manubrium	o Saggitari	4.4	Sun–Mars
Rukbat Al Rami, Nibat Anu	α Sagittarius		
Vega, Wega	α Lyra	0.14	Venus–Mercury

Place by (Sign)	Orb of Effect	10 Yr Shift (Mins)	Sidereal Place	Declin-ation	Cel. Lat.
28 SA 46	1°0′	9.9	4 SA 54	34S47	11S22
29 SA 34	1°40′	8.4	5 SA 46	9S46	13N41
0 CP 31	*1°0′*	*9.0*	*6 SA 42*	*23S26*	*0N01*
3 CP 06	1°30′	8.9	8 SA 30	21S05	2N21
6 CP 09	1°40′	8.4	11 SA 34	24S47	2S39
8 CP 14	1°0′	9.1	13 SA 38	23S58	0S43
12 CP 12	2°10′	8.4	17 SA 37	26S24	3S26
13 CP 27	2°0′	8.3	18 SA 52	30S00	7S10
14 CP 52	1°30′	8.4	20 SA 17	21S[illegible]2	0N52
conjunct with *Manubrium*					
15 CP 09	2°40′	8.5	20 SA 34	38N42	61N44

Star Name(s)	Constellation & Greek Letter	Vis. Mag.	Planet Simile
Deneb Al Ukhab *Dhanab Al Nasr* *Aquilae Cauda*	ζ Aquila	3.02	Mars–Jupiter
Terebellum	ω Sagittari	5.0	Venus–Saturn
Albireo	β Cygnus	3.24	Venus–Jupiter
Altair	α Aquila	0.6	Mars–Jupiter
Al Giedi *Al Jady*	α Capricorn	3.77	Venus –Mars
Al Shat	ν Capricorn		
Dabih	β Capricorn	3.25	Saturn –Venus
Oculus Capricorn	π Capr'n	5.0	Saturn – Venus
Bos	ρ Capricorn	5.0	Saturn –Venus
Al Bali	ε Aquarius	3.8	(Mars–Mercury)
Armus	η Capricorn	5.0	Mars–Mercury

Place by (Sign)	Orb of Effect	10 Yr Shift (Mins)	Sidereal Place	Declin-ation	Cel. Lat.
19 CP 37	1°40′	8.3	25 SA 02	13N45	36N12
25 CP 44	1°0′	8.4	1 CP 09	26S31	5S25
1 AQ 06	1°40′	8.4	6 CP 31	27N47	48N59
1 AQ 34	2°40′	8.0	6 CP 59	8N39	29N18
3 AQ 39	1°30′	8.3	9 CP 04	12S47	6N58

Conjunct with *Al Giedi*

3 AQ 53	1°40′	8.3	9 CP 18	15S02	4N36
4 AQ 34	1°0′	8.56	9 CP 58	18S29	0N54
5 AQ 02	1°0′	8.55	10 CP 26	18S05	1N12
10 AQ 45	1°40′	8.5	16 CP 11	8S13	7N56
12 AQ 35	1°0′	8.51	18 CP 00	20S10	2S59

Star Name(s)	Constellation & Greek Letter	Vis. Mag.	Planet Simile
Dorsum	θ Capricorn	5.0	Saturn –Jupiter
Castra	ϵ Capricorn	5.0	Saturn –Jupiter
Nashira	γ Capricorn	3.8	Saturn –Jupiter
Saad Al Suud	β Aquarius	3.07	Saturn –Mercury
Deneb Al Giedi	δ Capricorn	2.98	Saturn –Jupiter
Saad Al Malik *Sadalmelik*	α Aquarius	3.19	Saturn –Mercury
Fom Al Hut *Fomalhaut*	α Piscis- -Australis	1.29	Venus– Mercury
Deneb Adige	α Cygnus	1.26	Venus– Mercury
Sadakhbia *Sadachbia*	γ. Aquarius	3.8	Venus– Mercury
Skat	δ Aquarius	3.51	Saturn –Jupiter
Varuna *Gdor, Ekchousis*	λ Aquarius	3.8	Saturn –Jupiter
Achernar	α Eridanus	0.6	Jupiter

Place by (Sign)	Orb of Effect	10 Yr Shift (Mins)	Sidereal Place	Declin-ation	Cel. Lat.
13 AQ 41	1°0′	8.4	19 CP 06	17S34	0S36
20 AQ 02	1°0′	8.4	25 CP 27	19S50	4S58
21 AQ 36	1°30′	8.31	27 CP 01	17S01	2S33
23 AQ 10	1°40′	7.5	28 CP 36	5S58	8N37
23 AQ 20	1°40′	7.5	28 CP 46	16S29	2S35
3 PS 06	1°40′	7.3	8 AQ 32	0S43	10N39
3 PS 30	2°30′	7.0	8 AQ 56	30S03	21S08
4 PS 49	2°30′	6.1	10 AQ 16	45N00	59N55
6.PS 20	1°30′	6.0	11 AQ 46	3S04	8N18
8 PS 32	1°40′	7.1	13 AQ 58	16S15	8S11
10 PS 40	1°30′	6.8	16 AQ 12	17S30	9S24
15 PS 00	2°40′	4.1	20 AQ 28	57S39	59S22

Star Name(s)	**Constellation & Greek Letter**	**Vis. Mag.**	**Planet Simile**
Situla *Al Satl, Al Daluu*	χ Aquarius	5.5	Saturn –Jupiter
Al Samakah *Fomalsamakah*	β Pisces	4.5	Jupiter–Mercury
Markab	α Pegasus	2.57	Mars–Mercury
Scheat *Al Shiat*	β pegasus	2.61 (var)	Mars–Mercury

Place by (Sign)	Orb of Effect	10 Yr Shift (Mins)	Sidereal Place	Declin- ation	Cel. Lat.
16 PS 30	1°0′	5.0	21 AQ 56	16S30	10S20
18 PS 41	1°10′	5.1	24 AQ 07	3N55	8N52
23 PS 13	2°0′	7.0	28 AQ 39	14N46	19N24
28 PS 59	2°0′	6.7	4 PS 25	27N39	31N08

Bibliography

In the course of writing a volume such as this, one needs must take a rest now and then, and have a look at something else. But even in those moments, a line somewhere in a book ostensibly unconnected with one's labours may strike up a new thought that clarifies a matter which had been a block to further progress. To record each and every one of such books is a practical impossibility now, but what follows here is a list of books which were intentionally consulted, and which will repay the attention also of our readers. They are listed under sub-headings of the matters they deal with.

Astrology

The Power of Fixed Stars, J.E. Rigor; Astrology & Spiritual Publishers Inc., Hammond, Indiana, 1979.

Christian Astrology, William Lilly; Regulus Publishing Co.Ltd, London, U.K., 1985

The Sabian Symbols in Astrology, Marc E. Jones; Shambhala Publications Inc., Boulder, Col., 1978.

An Astrological Mandala, Dane Rudhyar; Vintage Books div., Random House, New York, 1974.

Astronomy

Collins Guide to Stars & Planets, Ridpath & Tirion; William Collins Ltd, Glasgow,U.K., 1984.

The Country Life Guide to Astronomy, Baker & Hardy; Country Life Books, Hamlyn Ltd, Feltham, U.K, 1982.

The Observer's Book of Astronomy, Patrick Moore; Frederick Warne & Co., London & New York, 1974.
Astronomy, A Dictionary of, Iain Nicolson; Arrow Books Ltd., London, U.K., 1977.
University Astronomy, Pasachoff & Kutner; W.B. Saunders Co., London, U.K., 1978.
The Intelligent Universe, Fred Hoyle; Michael Joseph Ltd., London, U.K., 1983

Folklore and History

Star Names, Their Lore & Meaning, R.H. Allen; Dover Publications, New York, 1963.
Hamlet's Mill, Santillana & von Dechend; David R. Godine Publs, Boston, Mass., 1983.
The Secret of Atlantis, Otto Muck; William Collins Ltd., Glasgow, U.K., 1978.
The Book of Lilith, Barbar B. Koltuv; Nicolas-Hays Inc., York Beach, Maine, 1986.
Man and His Symbols, Carl G. Jung; Aldus Books Ltd., London, U.K., 1964.

Religious Sources

The Holy Bible, King James Edition.
The Quran, Translation by Sir Muhammad Zafrullah Khan, Curzon Press, London, U.K, 1971.

General Reference

Encyclopedia Britannica.
Brockhaus Encyclopedia.
Larousse Encyclopedia.

Postscript

After four years of assembling notes, I began the writing of this book in July 1987, promising my publisher that I would hand over the completed manuscript at the end of October. But in late August strange events led to me marrying again in the following month, then bearing with my dear new wife, Kimmi's departure to a Greater World than this, taking with her our beloved friend Poppy.

All work on this book stopped for six months, but another may yet be written if God so Wills it, on the extraordinary and wonderful experiences which the two of them, and others, brought to me, and to others, upon their rebirth into New Life. It has been new life also for all of us who have been privileged to be a part of those experiences, and our gratitude to God, by whatever Name we may call Him, is boundless.

During those months, right from the first day, and still now, I have been supported and encouraged by a legion of newly-found friends from as far apart as Canada and Pakistan, and many lands between them.

I have been especially blessed by Arab friends of Kimmi and Poppy, and others who came to know of them later. These have gathered around me, not only with great sympathy but also with practical help, searching through works of Al Biruni, Al Akhsassi, Tazwini and others whose classics I could not read for myself. They have also taught me to begin the mastery of their language for myself, so vital to the completion of this book.

Many of these hold positions in Religion, State, Industry and Science which oblige them to remain anonymous to readers, as must such people anywhere in the world, for it is still largely 'not done' for ministers and managers in the exoteric affairs of the world to publicise their intelligent interest in the esoteric side of life. Yet they are so many in number that some day in the future we, and they, will be astonished to find that whole hosts of them were engaged in the pursuit of deep wisdom, keeping it modestly secret from each other!

There is an irony in that, but let there be no hint of mockery. Those people must work in the world as it is, if they are to fufill the missions they hold in trust for us. Because they have found deeper wisdom, they know they must await the right time to tell all that they know, at the time when the world is ready to hear and believe them.

Unpublished though their names must be, I give them all my heartfelt thanks for the warmth and help which not one of them was obliged to come forward and give, save at the command of that Greater Source of Wisdom to which their own faith and diligence has led them.

A final word to my readers. If on reading this book you find items of interest, pleasure and stimulation to your thoughts and hearts, then I am happy. That, more than all else, is what I wrote this book for.

There must be errors in a work of this length, and you will do me a kindness by pointing them out to me. There are, I hope, ideas which can be developed further between us, and I shall be pleased to hear from anyone who wishes to carry on the discussion which has begun here.

Eric Morse, London, June, 1988

Index of Stars and Constellations

Note: The Arabic article Al (sometimes El) has generally been included in names but does not determine their alphabetic order. Thus, for example, *Al Nath* appears under N, while *Al Wasat* is under W. Where more than one page/chapter reference is given, the first is the most important.